During one of the most emotional
history, Clenora Hudson-Weems' _
Presidential Candidacy of Barack Ob
regarding his historic quest. Using he. ....., ... as a reference
point, Clenora discusses such phenomena as the Democratic primary battle between
Obama & Hillary Clinton, & the role of Michelle Obama, which courageously
illuminates how race & gender continue to be "hot button" issues in American society.
Robert E. Weems, Jr., PhD, Professor of History (UMC); author--*Desegregating the
Dollar: African American Consumerism in the 20th Century; Business in Black & White:
American Presidents & Black Entrepreneurs in the 20th Century*

Written with passion & grace, this timely volume represents both summa & extension
of Hudson-Weems' lifetime of passionate social theorizing & activist advancement of
Africana Womanism. Part social theory, part literary discourse, part sermon, & part
political commentary, these essays send forth a Call & blueprint for the spiritual healing
of Africana male-female-family-community. Here we find Clenora's bold counterforce
to the historic race & class limitations of an Anglo-American individual rights-based
feminism. It is in this Africana Womanist vision that she sets out not only the pre-
conditions for a healed black femininity & black America, but for all international
peoples of color & for our own still racially-riven nation. Coming on the eve of an
historic election, featuring the very 1st African American presidential candidate, this
book situates itself in the next great watershed moment for Blacks and for the nation
itself.
Gloria L. Cronin, PhD, Author and Professor of English, Brigham Young University

This is truly a significant book for Africana scholars & the American public alike.
Hudson-Weems provides us with powerful writings that chronicle the evolution of
Africana Womanism from its critical philosophies she outlined in the mid-eighties, to
its applicability as a complex socio-political rubric for deconstructing contemporary
issues of race & gender. Obama, the first Black presidential nominee in the 2008
democratic primaries, & Michelle can be better understood within the construct
of improved race relations & a better society with the urgent need to discard petty
prejudices based purely upon racial & gender differences.
E. Lincoln James, PhD, Professor, Chief Editor, *Western Journal of Black Studies,*
Washington State University.

Dr. Clenora Hudson–Weems' book is an important & timely contribution to the
continuing discourse on feminism, African Feminism, womanism & Africana
womanism. While all aim to advance the democratization process, Africana Womanism
focuses more on the experiences & struggles of Black families in the African Diaspora
& in Africa as a whole & on social justice. This book will be an important resource
for academics & students in Africana Studies, Women's Studies, the Social Sciences
& Humanities. It is also a good reference and mobilizing tool for activists and policy
makers interested in strengthening the global Africana family & the global society.
Filomina Chioma Steady, PhD, Author, Professor & Chair, Dept. of Africana Studies-
-Wellesley College

I like the profound honesty in which Clenora's writings present truth. *Africana Womanism & Race & Gender in the Presidential Candidacy of Barack Obama* is so dynamic. It is simply stated and right on target. The struggles between the genders are very apparent and have always been a hot topic. Coming from a background that deals with beauty, fashion and the media, I have seen first hand how powerfully destructive these industries have been in the lives of not only Africana sisters & brothers but others as well. Nonetheless there has to be some balance so that we can get back in touch with who we truly are, a critical step in more effectively incorporating into the broader base of positive race & gender relations in general.
Antoinette Alexander Sarpong, Founder, President, CEO, Antoinette Assoc Inc & YOU'I Global Co.

This is a racist country, as racist as South Africa was, built on the backs of slaves. The mentality and primal thinking of the American masses are racist, but only 3 out of 10 will admit it. It's like a big elephant in the room that no one wants to admit it. Until we publically talk about it, we will forever be stuck in this mentality, unable to heal and transform our country. By the same token, the American society is sexist, built into the fabric of our society; women are 2nd class citizens. A timely book, exploring the current political racist and sexist dynamics in a productive and healing way, it closes with the hope of redemption for possible racial harmony and economic salvation.
Sandy Kravitz-Reid, Civil Rights Activist and Businesswoman, Los Angeles, CA

Dr. Hudson Weems, a champion, who creates champions of us all, has had a great impact on my perception of life. When introduced to Africana Womanism, I instantly began to blow the trumpet of her mission, sharing with the world its relevancy. To reclaim, rename, redefine & assert ourselves is vital to the survival of our race. This book will support, nurture & sustain your desire to reclaim your stake & rightful place in history. Join the many Africana people around the globe who are rebuilding family structure, designing community platforms & refining the foundation of a nation. Clenora is hosting a world party via the Africana Womanist Society & "It's a Family Affair."
Jibril Serapis Bey, Music Artist, Song Writer (www.africanawomanism.com)

In this book, the professor shows her passion for interpreting and correcting things affecting the overall conditions of our society. This is a continuation of everything I have known her to do in her research activities. For instance, she joined me in my 20-year battle for my daughter, a disabled American citizen, to write our book to right the wrongs Denise suffered. Likewise she started her 20-year Emmett Till (also disabled) research to correct the omission of the importance of his lynching to the American public. Now she is highlighting the importance of the American people to turn their backs on all forms of discrimination by putting their confidence in Barack Obama, the 1st Black U.S. presidential candidate.
Dora Anderson, co-author with Clenora Hudson-Weems of *The Rosa Parks of the Disabled Movement*

Africana Womanism & Race & Gender in the Presidential Candidacy of Barack Obama

Clenora Hudson-Weems, PhD

FOREWORD BY
Rev. Lennox Yearwood Jr.
President and CEO, Hip Hop Caucus

AFTERWORD BY
Atty. Alvin O. Chambliss, Jr.
"Last Original Civil Rights Attorney in America"

Parity

authorHOUSE®

AuthorHouse™
1663 Liberty Drive, Suite 200
Bloomington, IN 47403
www.authorhouse.com
Phone: 1-800-839-8640

First published by AuthorHouse 8/21/2008

ISBN: 978-1-4389-0327-9 (sc)
ISBN: 978-1-4389-0906-6 (hc)

Front Cover photo provided and used with permission of Getty Images

Library of Congress Control Number: 2008906712

Printed in the United States of America
Bloomington, Indiana

This book is printed on acid-free paper.

Parity

authorHOUSE®

OTHER WORKS BY THE AUTHOR

The Rosa Parks of the Disabled Movement: Plantation Politics & a Black Woman's Struggle against GM, UAW & Government Bureaucrats (co-author, Dora Anderson) AuthorHouse, Parity, 2008

Contemporary Africana Theory, Thought & Action: A Guide to Africana Studies, Africa World Press, 2007

Plagiarism—Physical & Intellectual Lynchings: An Emmett Till Continuum, AuthorHouse, Parity, 2007

The Definitive Emmett Till: Passion & Battle of a Woman for Truth & Intellectual Justice, AuthorHouse, Parity, 2006

Emmett Till: The Sacrificial Lamb of the Civil Rights Movement AuthorHouse, Parity, 2006

Africana Womanist Literary Theory, Africa World Press, 2004

Emmett Till: The Sacrificial Lamb of the Civil Rights Movement Bedford, 1994

Africana Womanism: Reclaiming Ourselves, Bedford, 1993

Toni Morrison (Co-Author with Dr. Wilfred D. Samuels, U. of Utah), Prentice Hall, 1990

Soul Mates, a novel, Forthcoming

American Audio Prose Library, Interview with author, Till & Africana
    Womanism, 1995

DEDICATION

*To my mother, Mary Person, my model Africana Womanist; my husband,
Robert, my model Africana Male Counterpart, and Cameron*

I dedicate this book to all of us and celebrate the anticipation of all, men,
women, and children, who commit themselves to a unified struggle.
Moreover, all Africana people must have a responsibility to each other,
and particularly to our children, our future generations, so that the rich
legacy of true Africana womanhood, for the survival of ourselves, our
male counterparts and moreover, our children as collective warriors in
the battle for our birthright as determiners of our fate and freedom, can
live on. Pass it on!

In memory of 14-year-old Emmett Louis "Bobo" Till (1941-1955),
whose August 28, 1955 brutal lynching was the true catalyst of the Civil
Rights Movement of the '50s and '60s ("Emmett Till: The Impetus of
the Modern Civil Rights Movement," 1988 Ford Doctoral Dissertation,
University of Iowa).

ACKNOWLEDGEMENTS

First, I would like to thank Africa World Press for permission to reprint two chapters ("Genuine Sisterhood or Lack Thereof" and "Africana Male-Female Relationships and Sexism in the Community") from *Africana Womanist Literary Theory*, and Chapter One ("Nommo/Self Naming, Self-Defining and the History of Africana Womanism") from *Contemporary Africana Theory, Thought and Action*. I also thank Bedford Publishers for the opportunity to expound upon one of the seminal chapters in *Africana Womanism: Reclaiming Ourselves*, Chapter Four, on the elements of the Africana Woman. I am eternally grateful to *The Western Journal of Black Studies*, the umbrella journal for Black Studies, founded in the seventies by Editor and Professor Emeritus of Washington State University, Talmadge Anderson, for not only the venue for my first publication on the subject in 1989, but for permission to reprint that seminal piece, "Cultural and Agenda Conflicts in Academia: Critical Issues for Africana Women's Studies." Finally, I wish to thank all brave Africana women, particularly those in the Academy, who dare to reassess our name, thereby defining ourselves and our action in a world that too frequently ostracizes us because of our status as non-traditionalists/main-streamers. Your many works and acts of identifying yourselves as Africana womanists speak volumes of your commitment to our people. I am also appreciative of the strong, authentic Africana men who acknowledge authentic Africana women both "in thought and in action" and recognize them as such in their support, particularly in the Academy, by upholding their position as Africana womanist scholars. The late Dr. C. Eric Lincoln, Professor Emeritus, Duke University, was such a supporter, as he proudly endorsed my first book on the subject, *Africana Womanism: Reclaiming Ourselves* in 1993. In describing me and my authentic scholarly activities, he made the following assertion, which I will continue to honor and uphold:

> *Africana Womanism sent unaccustomed shock waves through the domain of popular thinking about feminism and established her as a careful thinker, unafraid to unsettle settled opinion. In Emmett Till, she drops the other shoe and challenges the most sacred shibboleths of the origins of the Civil Rights Movement. Not everyone will want to agree with what she has to say. But few will lay the book down before she has had her say. And she says America needs to hear again right now.*
> *(Lincoln, Emmett Till: The Sacrificial Lamb of the Civil Rights Movement, Jacket blurb, 1993).*

Contents

FOREWORD

Historically, Africana women have wanted to be "liberated" to the community, family, and its responsibilities. The daily evacuation of males and females from the Africana community in a nine-to-five society has wreaked havoc on the sense of security of Africana children. The distress of these Africana children and their need for comforting seem to have been ignored, overlooked and vastly underplayed, suggesting that these children do not need this kind of support. The result is generations of hurt and rejection.

(HUDSON-WEEMS, AFRICANA WOMANISM, 34)

Dr. Clenora Hudson-Weems is profound in her discourse, as she thoroughly explores the tuning dimensions of the African American woman and the struggles she endures to assert her dual identity. It is necessary that one observes Africana Womanism, a theory both named and defined by Dr. Hudson-Weems, as a concept essential to improving the African American lifestyle for men, women and children, particularly within, though not limited to, the urban landscape. The cycle of poverty, homelessness, street violence, and drug wars is presumed to be impenetrable, yet Dr. Hudson-Weems gives us hope with the concept of reinstituting values of respect, equality, and empowerment for all, both Africana men and women. By delineating the invaluable characteristics that engender the African American woman in particular, we better understand how crucial the mother figure is to, what I call, the Hip Hop generation. This generation is comprised of young people in need of the opportunity to express their minds and actively speak out for their respective causes in the socio-political arena, and they use Hip Hop as a tool to create such an opportunity.

One of the biggest obstacles for many within this new generation is the absence of women in the lives of their children, as they make priority out of their careers. Although there is obviously nothing wrong with the professional empowerment of women, there needs to be a balance, as Africana womanism calls for in one of the eighteen characteristic of Africana Womanism, the flexible role player. She is not only worker, but mother and ideally spouse, too, thereby making possible the restoration of the holistic mother figure in the lives of American youths. It is important to note that the problem of the absentee father is also devastating to the youth and likewise must be addressed and corrected if at all possible. Particularly within the urban landscape, the absence of parental guidance, as Hudson-Weems discusses in her book, has consequentially led to gangs as a substitute parent. There also needs to be more persistency among the youth to revive the original agenda of Hip Hop and redefine the way women are perceived in mainstream Hip Hop culture. Misogyny and female subjugation are critical issues, which are unfortunately prevalent in Hip Hop culture due to its commercialization. This is where Africana Womanism is very effective, if implemented as a universal concept.

As the book moves more prominently from a personal to a political stance, such as the case of the current presidential election discussed in the last chapter of the book, "Racism versus Classism/Obama versus Clinton: Human Survival/Economic Security—Unity or Gender Divide," the role of the woman, the wife of the first African American Democratic nominee, Michelle, is highly significance. In much the same way that the woman should operate in any arena, here she must be true to her sense of family-centerness, and particularly in this circumstance, as co-partner to her mate, supporting a traditional Africana womanist way of sharing and participating in each other's needs for success and survival. In the final analysis, it is evident that women are key figures in Hip Hop culture, too, as they have the power to revitalize its purpose as a civil and human rights agenda that can be embodied in not only their personal lives, but more important, in a dynamic socio-political diverse racial, cultural, and class progressive movement as well.

REV. LENNOX YEARWOOD JR.

PRESIDENT AND CEO, HIP HOP CAUCUS

(WWW.HIPHOPCAUCUS.ORG)

PREFACE

An Africana womanist . . . is a black woman activist who is family centered rather than female centered and who focuses on race and class empowerment before gender empowerment.

(HILL, CALL AND RESPONSE, P. 1379)

In the above quotation, which appears in the head-notes to the section of the anthology, entitled "Women's Voices of Self-Definition," the general editor of *Call and Response: The Riverside Anthology of the African American Literary Theory*, Patricia Liggings Hill, takes a positive, bold stand on the agenda of the Africana womanist, which, while it is not anti-feminist, is certainly not feminist. That authentic agenda for all women of African descent, which the selections in this volume highlight, strongly parallels my evolution from student to teacher, which is made clear to me as I reflect on my last five years in academe.

There are many instances in our lives when The Creator allows us to experience His glorious and wondrous works. There is no doubt that He is the progenitor of every pleasant thought and action. It is my personal belief that God uses people to fulfill His divine purpose. I feel that Dr. Clenora Hudson-Weems, a dynamic woman of God, is the embodiment of the Africana Womanist, which includes spirituality as one of the eighteen (18) features of Africana Womanism. In so many ways, the concept of Africana Womanism is her personal ministry and she continues to use it as a means of enriching and even changing the lives of other people. A dynamic speaker, Dr. Hudson-Weems is a phenomenal scholar, who has the rare and unique ability to captivate her audiences and her students by just keeping it real. She skillfully intertwines her teaching abilities with unconditional love, corrective candor, tender generosity and rare humor.

I first met Dr. Hudson-Weems at the College Language Association National Conference in Washington, D.C. in April 2003. At the time, my mentor and Chair of my Master's thesis, Dr. Betty Taylor-Thompson, introduced me to Dr. Hudson-Weems, who talked very openly with me about my future academic and professional goals. She asked if I would be interested in applying to the Ph.D. program at MU in English with a concentration in Africana Literary Theory and Thought. I gleefully exclaimed, "Yes, Ma'am" and assured her that when I returned to Houston, I would apply. Although I had missed the deadline for admissions, the Graduate School, upon learning that I was Dr. Hudson-Weems' recruit, urged me to send my application materials to them immediately. I soon realized that something beautiful and miraculous had just occurred---a critically acclaimed author, scholar, educator, theorist, and motivational speaker had just invited *me* to study under her. I was accepted to the university in June of 2003. Although she was on leave during my first semester at the university, Dr. Hudson-Weems called to check on me weekly, just as any good mother would do. Clearly she was playing the role of more that just my mentor. She even called my professors periodically to check on my progress.

During the spring semester of 2004, I had the pleasure of enrolling in both her "Africana Womanism" and "Africana Male Writers" classes, which were in great demand, as students, both Black and white, were always there requesting overrides into the classes. Her lectures were always engaging and insightful. I often told her that her classes were better than Monday night football because one never knew what to expect in her classes. We read and discussed her ground-breaking work, *Africana Womanism: Reclaimimg Ourselves*, which changed the way that many of us viewed ourselves and feminism. She emphasized the application of the eighteen tenets of Africana Womanism to five (5) select novels--Zora Neale Hurston's *Their Eyes Were Watching God*, Mariama Bâ's *So Long a Letter*, Paule Marshall's *Praisesong for the Widow*, Toni Morrison's *Beloved*, and Terry McMillan's *Disappearing Acts*. Her students, particularly those of African descent, were able to truly understand the foundation of the theory of Africana Womanism, which was the prioritization of race, class, and gender. The white students, too, were clearer on the applicability of Africana womanist theory to Black life, and thus, were able to step outside of their cultural context in considering Black texts and experiences.

There were many instances after class when my classmates and I would talk about Africana Womanism and we would marvel at its relevance to our lives. Many of us saw ourselves blossom during that semester. Dr. Hudson-Weems' scholarship had left an indelible mark on our lives and for me in particular on both my personal and academic life. Her courses have enabled me to experience a remarkable spiritual renaissance. In so many ways, I had been, as they say in many of the African American churches, born again. Africana Womanism encouraged me to explore and celebrate my own cultural history. I now see the beauty that lies in authentic Africana theories. I appreciate the fact that their value is not only limited to the classroom, but that they can be applied to real life situations and relationships as well. Thus, Africana Womanism teaches us how to rebuild our families, our relationships with one another, our spiritual lives and our communities.

After taking those two courses, I became an Africana Womanist fanatic. I wanted and needed to enroll in every course that Hudson-Weems taught because it empowered me as a Black person on a predominately white campus. Thanks to Dr. Hudson-Weems and Africana Womanism, I was able to truly exist without apology and truly enjoy my Africanness. In the fall of 2004, I enrolled in her Africana Literary Theory course, which was a God-Sent for Africana Womanist junkies like myself. My understanding of myself and the collective struggle of our ancestors continued to grow. There was no question as to what the subject of my dissertation would be. I was honored to write my dissertation on a concept that I loved so dearly and I was equally honored when Hudson-Weems agreed to direct my doctoral dissertation. The dissertation, which was entitled, "Claiming/Reclaiming Africana Womanist Literary Text throughout the African Diaspora," articulated the need for Africana people to create our own theories in order that we may better be able to accurately define ourselves. I used Africana Womanism as the primary tool of analysis and applied it to literary works that spanned the African American, African Caribbean, and African literary traditions.

In May 2006, I became the Nation's first student to receive a Ph.D. in English with an Africana Concentration (Africana Literature, Criticism and Theory), a new emphasis in English, which was conceptualized and designed by Dr. Hudson-Weems. She told me that it was after announcing this concentration in 2002 that she became active in recruiting students into the department. As I prepared for the ceremony, I was sad, happy and excited all at the same time. I was sad because I was leaving Columbia and my spiritual family at the Second Baptist Church. Most important, I was leaving a woman who had mothered, mentored and protected me from many of the world's horrors. As I marched in with my class, I reflected on our travels together. When she was invited to speak at the University of Hamburg in Germany, Dr. Hudson-Weems invited me to join her. I was so amazed and honored. She was a plenary speaker on her works on both Africana Womanism and Emmett Till and the receptivity of her work was astounding. The time that we spent in Amsterdam and Hamburg are among my favorite and most cherished memories. I remember our trip to my mother's wedding in Houston, TX, as well as our trips to her hometown, Memphis, TN. I was happy and excited about finishing because I knew both my family and Dr. Hudson-Weems were elated; she told me how pleased she was with my work. I was confident, knowing that she had equipped me with the tools that I needed to be successful. Because she empowered me with knowledge, self-awareness and love, I was excited about the many directions that my professional and personal lives were beginning to take.

Upon graduation, I returned to my hometown, Houston, Texas, taking a teaching position at my Alma Mater, Texas Southern University I work daily to empower my students, just as Dr. Hudson-Weems had done and would expect of me. I view teaching as my personal ministry and I know that God allows me to use it also as a vehicle for touching people's lives. Although Dr. Hudson-Weems is not with me in Houston, I still strive to make her proud of me by continuing her legacy and commitment to Africana people. I talk to my students about Africana Womanism and the need for them to respect and love themselves, as well as their neighbors. Africana Womanism has not only helped my career, my love life as well has flourished because of it. The concept has enhanced my understanding of the daily struggles that the Africana male continues to face. On July 6, 2007, I married a man who truly complements me. He is the physical manifestation of the positive and strong Africana male characteristics which Dr. Hudson-Weems described in her work. In short, he understands all too well the critical need for the Africana man and woman to respect and love each other so that we can build solid families together for the survival of our future generations. Like the subtitle of Chapter IX of *Africana Womanism* on Terri McMillan's *Disappearing Acts* asserts, we are all "in it together." And this is most definitely the case of all Americans that Dr. Hudson-Weems closes this book with regarding the case of Presidential Candidate, Barack Obama, his wife, Michelle and their family, and moreover, the entire American people .

LINDA JOHNSON-BURGESS, PHD

DEPARTMENT OF ENGLISH, TEXAS SOUTHERN UNIVERSITY

Introduction

The first African American woman intellectual to formulate a position on Africana womanism was Clenora Hudson-Weems, author of the 1993 groundbreaking study Africana Womanism: Reclaiming Ourselves. . . . Of all the theoretical models, Hudson-Weems's best describes the racially based perspective of many black women's rights advocates, beginning with Maria W. Stewart and Frances W. Harper in the early nineteenth century.

(Hill, Call and Response 1379, 1811)

One of the most important endorsements of Africana Womanism I could have received came from the most powerful and widely used anthologies in the Academy, *Call and Response: the Riverside Anthology in the African American Literary Tradition* (1998), a Houghton Mifflin signature edition. *Call and Response* strongly echoes the authenticity of an earlier Black Aesthetic anthology, *Black Writers of America: A Comprehensive Anthology* (1972), published by McMillan Publishing Company, which was co-edited by my mentor, the late Dr. Richard K. Barksdale, and Keneth Kinnamon, who taught me the true meaning of authenticity.

Africana Womanism and Race and Gender in the Presidential Candidacy of Barack Obama, my third book (trilogy) on the subject, evolved from two main demands: First is the need to synthesize some of the best of my writings on Africana Womanism during the last two decades, and secondly, the need to introduce new ideas, reflecting the continuing concerns inherent in the growing body of the Africana Womanist school of thought and the tendencies relative to information on the dynamics of interpersonal relationships as we move more prominently into the political arena. This volume demonstrates the applicability of Africana Womanism as a useful tool for assessing political activity, particularly the

9

current historical presidential election surrounding the Nation's very first Black nominee for the Democratic Party for the President of the United States of America, Senator Barack Obama. Within this paradigm, unity becomes the ultimate objective, for it is only when we come together that we become able to receive the beauty of life, happiness and success.

Chapter One, "Cultural and Agenda Conflicts in Academia: Critical Issues for Africana Women's Studies," is a reprint, which is crucial, as it was the very first publication, 1989, on the subject in which I called for a new name and paradigm for Africana women throughout the world. Chapter Two, "Nommo, Self-Naming, Self-Defining, and the History of Africana Womanism," a synthesis of Chapter One of *Africana Womanism: Reclaiming Ourselves* (1993), and other published articles and book chapters on the subject, introduces evolving ideas on this very provocative subject, as additional ideas grew out of the Question and Answer Sessions during the numerous speaking engagements and conference papers I delivered over the years. Chapter Three, "The Eighteen (18) Descriptors for the Africana Womanist," grew out of Chapter Four of the original text, expanding on the eighteen characteristics of the Africana womanist. Chapter Four, "The Africana Womanist's Male Counterpart" is a seminal chapter, which highlights the true nature of the true Africana man, always in concert with the Africana woman. This is a new development for the paradigm, which was only introduced in the conclusion of *Africana Womanism*. Chapter Five, "Genuine Sisterhood or Lack Thereof" and Chapter Six, "Africana Male-Female Relationships and Sexism in the Community," grew out of constant requests from many for me to expound further on these critical issues, reflecting three of the characteristics of the true Africana womanist (Genuine Sisterhood, Male-Female Compatibility, and In Concert with Male in Struggle) as defined. Chapter Seven, "In Response to Don Imus, 2007: Anti-Misogyny in Defense of Africana Women," reflects my immediate reaction to the outrageous disrespect of Black women by Don Imus on his nationally-syndicated talk show, *Imus in the Morning*, a subject that has become frequently brought up in the media, particularly regarding rap music. The subject of this chapter draws into the dialogue people from both inside and outside the Academy, as well it should, for it is critical that the theory connects at all times with the broader community at large, thereby remaining a subject of debate and consideration for all.

Chapter Eight, entitled "Racism versus Sexism/Obama versus Clinton: Human Survival/Economic Security—Unity or Gender Divide," brings the book to a close on a political note. Africana Womanism, like any other viable concept, by its very nature, must continue to expand, as it must draw into the debate issues impacting upon all fronts. Specifically in the case of Obama, the very fact that he is Black and has been favored by God and the American people alone signifies an in-place structure for possible solutions to social ills, particularly life-threatening issues due to racist and sexist mentalities, let alone his platform for improving economic and war related problems. The final chapter, the Conclusion—"Authentic Existence, Racial Healing and Economic Security"--recapitulates the ideals of Africana Womanism and applies them to the current political activities, including the current presidential election. Atty. Alvin O. Chambliss, Jr. wraps the book up in the Afterword, in which he comments on the urgency of the political spend on all things relative to humankind. Unquestionably, these things indelibly impact on life itself, relative to our freedom and our birth-right to a quality and fair existence as "fellow citizens," consisting of both seasoned and budding Africana womanists and their male counterparts. His commentary is followed by Charlotte Gibson-Bauer, Emmy Award-Winning television writer and playwright, in the Epilogue, which leaves us with the hope of restoring the image of America via the mission and legacy of hope that Barack and his female counterpart, his wife Michelle, hold for all of us.

It should be noted here that there is also a growing number of Africana Womanist societies throughout the country. Women, and even some men, are finding their niche within this construct because of its applicability to their lives in both the workplace and the home place. Dr. Alma Vinyard, Chair of the Department of English at Clark Atlanta University, where I received my Master's Degree under the tutorage of Dr. Richard Barksdale, Dean of the Graduate School of Arts and Sciences, and Lucy Grigsby, Chair of the Department of English at the Atlanta University, was present at the launching of the Africana Womanist Society in Pittsburgh. In the Foreword to the Forth Revised Edition of *Africana Womanism Literary Theory*, Dr. Vinyard contends that

> *Since first meeting and hearing Clenora Hudson-Weems speak at an international conference at the University of Nigeria-*

11

Nsukka in 1992 to the present, . . . I have witnessed the powerful evolution of Africana Womanism from theory to practice. On the academic front, Africana Womanism: Reclaiming Ourselves has been acclaimed in many scholarly citations, . . . However, the academic component is only a part oft this phenomenal concept. It has gone far beyond the halls of academe, represented in major texts . . . Africana Womanism reaches fruition in the public arena, validated by the launching of the Charter Chapter of the Africana Womanist Society in Pittsburgh, PA in the fall of 2004. This momentous tribute established Africana Womanism as a contemporary holistic movement for all women of African descent in concert with Africana men (Vinyard, quoted in Africana Womanism , xi).

To be sure, Africana Womanism is growing and expanding its base from thought to action, as all authentic Africana theoretical ideas and constructs must do, which is significantly indicated in its expansion to the political sphere in this book. As announced at the very outset of the ascendance of Africana Womanism, "the primary goal of Africana women, then, is to create their own criteria for assessing their realities, both in thought and in action" (Hudson-Weems, *Africana Womanism*, 50). The realities are both vast and ever growing. Central to the quotation is the unique and authentic agenda, significantly different from any other female-based theoretical construct and more important, it is its continuing growth, development and applicability both inside and outside the Academy that keep this authentic theory so very much alive and in demand.

PART I

Africana Womanism: Its History and Its Features (Male & Female)

For the Black woman in a racist society, racial factors, rather that sexual ones, operate more consistently in making her a target for discrimination and marginalization. This becomes apparent when the "family" is viewed as a unit of analysis. Regardless of differential access to resources by both men and women, white males and females, as members of family groups, share a proportionately higher quantity of the earth's resources than do Black males and females. There is a great difference between discrimination by privilege and protection, and discrimination by deprivation and exclusion.

(Filomina Chioma Steady, The Black Woman

Cross-Culturally, 27-28)

Chapter One

Cultural and Agenda Conflicts in Academia: Critical Issues for Africana Women's Studies

Well, chillum, whar dar is so much racket, dar must be something out o' kilter. I t'ink dat 'twixt de niggers of de Souf [both men and women] an' de women at de Norf' all a--talkin' bout rights, de white men will be n a fix pretty soon. But what's all dis here talkin' about?

Dat man ober dar say dat women needs to be helped into carriages, and lifted ober ditches, and to have de best place everywhere.... Nobody eber helped me into carriages, or ober mud puddles, or give me any best place! And aren't I a Woman? [The issue is her blackness-and-race not her womanhood that has caused her to be excluded.] Look at me. Look at my arm. I have plowed and planted and gathered into barns and not man could head me-- and aren't I a woman? I have born'd five children and seen 'em mos' all sold off into slavery, and when I cried out with mother's grief, none but Jesus heard...and aren't I a woman?

Den dey talks 'bout dis t'ing in de head--what dis dey call it? Dat's it, honey--intellect....Now, What's dat got to do wit women's rights or niggers' rights [two separate groups who share the commonality of oppression]? If my cup won't hold but a pint

*and yourn holds a quart, wouldn't ye be mean not to let me have
my little half-measure full?*
*Den dat little man in black dar, he say women can't have as
much rights as man, 'cause Christ warn't a woman....Whar
did your Christ come from? Whar did your Christ come from?
From God and a woman! Man had nothing to do with him! If
de fust woman God ever made was strong enough to turn the
world upside down, all alone--dese togedder ought to be able to
turn it back and get it rightside up again; and now dey is asking
to do it, de men better let 'em. Bleeged to ye for hearin' on me;
and now ole Sojourner hain't got nothing more to say. (Hill,
261-2)*

During her lifetime as a staunch upholder of truth and justice,
Sojourner Truth, born a slave in 1797 and freed under the 1827 New
York Sate Emancipation Act, often unexpectedly appeared at antislavery
and women's rights rallies. Her impromptu remarks often - times served
to refute antagonistic arguments against both her race and her sex - and
in that order. Her frequently quoted speech above, which was both
unsolicitedly delivered and, because of her color, initially unwelcomed
by the white audience at an 1852 Woman's Rights Convention in Akron,
Ohio, is used here to demonstrate the critical position of the Africana
woman within the context of the modern feminist movement.

Historically, Africana women have fought against sexual
discrimination, as well as race and class discrimination; they have, indeed,
challenged Africana male chauvinism, but not to the extent of eliminating
Africana men as allies in the struggle for liberation and familihood. To
be sure, historically, Africana women have wanted to be "liberated" to the
community, family, and its responsibilities; for the evacuation of males
and females in the Africana community from nine to five has alarmingly
reeked havoc on the sense of security of Africana children left behind in
that community. Consequently, in the absence of parental guidance and
discipline, gangs, often become the substitute parent. But somehow over
the years, the distress of and need for comforting Africana children seem
to have been ignored, overlooked, and vastly underplayed, suggesting
that these children do not require this kind of support. The result is
generations of hurt and rejection. Even Africana women, who happen

to be on welfare and are perhaps at home, are condemned for not having a job and thus are often regarded as negative figure sin the sense that they do not offer an adult presence. With polarized minds, Africanans have bought into this view, embracing all too frequently the stereotype of the Africana woman on welfare and the disapproval of it. Nevertheless, Africana women are seeking to reclaim security, stability, and nurturing of a family-based community.

According to Vivian Gordon in *Black Women, Feminism and Black Liberation: Which Way?*:

> *To address women's issues, therefore, is not only to address the crucial needs of Black women, it is also to address the historic primacy of the African and African American community; that is, the primacy of its children and their preparation for the responsibilities and privileges of mature personhood. (viii)*

Hence, Africana women have historically demonstrated that they are diametrically opposed to the concept of many white feminists who want independence and freedom from family responsibilities. In the Statement of Purpose that the National Organization of Women (NOW) issued in 1966 and still issues today, "...it is no longer either necessary or possible for women to devote the greater part of their lives to child rearing..." Apparently, the motivating factor of many of these women is the desire to be liberated from the family. Others take it a step farther in their desire to be liberated from the obligation to men in particular; this sentiment, of course, may appeal more to radical lesbian or to radical feminist separatists. It is too often the case that many white feminists deny traditional familihood as a paramount part of their personal and professional lives.

All too frequently, Sojourner's resounding query "And aren't I a women?" is extrapolated from the text in order to force feminist identification on the speaker without any initial or even later reference to her first obstacle, race. In fact, as indicated on the occasion of Sojourner's speech, white's had not even deemed her as human, let alone as a woman, which is precisely why she was mocked before they finally allowed her to speak. One may question what this has to do with the modern feminist movement? The fact is that these racist perceptions have not changed significantly enough to suggest that Africana women do not yet have to contend with the same problem of insidious racism with almost equal intensity even though it is somewhat masked today.

In attempting to unearth historical truths about the feminist movement that divide white feminists from black feminists, Hazel V. Carby asserts that:

> *In order to gain a public voice as orators or published writers, black women had to confront the dominant domestic ideologies and literary conventions of womanhood which exclude them from the definition "woman." (Carby 6)*

Moreover, many have farcically used Sojourner's quotation to justify labeling this freedom fighter as a feminist or a "pre-feminist." White feminists often impose their interpretation of the Africana experience when it is convenient; for them, Sojourner's experience became a dramatization of female oppression. Ironically, Sojourner was attacking rather than embracing an element of the women's rights agenda that excluded her. Instead of aligning herself with the feminist cause, she was engaging in self-actualization, forcing white feminists, in particular, to recognize her and all Africana women as women and as a definite and legitimate part of that community. Furthermore, she was politically critiquing and defining herself and her movement. During the abolitionist movement white women learned techniques from the Africana women that would enable them to organize, to hold public meetings, and to conduct petition campaigns. As abolitionists, the white women first learned to speak in public and then began to formulate a philosophy to manifest their basic rights and their place in society. Africana women, on the other hand, had learned and practiced all these things centuries ago, from traditions in their Motherland.

But procrusteans have mislabeled Africana women activists like Sojourner Truth, along with other prominent Africana women freedom fighters such as Harriet Tubman (who spent her life aiding Africana slaves, both males and females, in their escape through the Underground Railroad to the North for freedom), and Ida B. Wells (an anti-lynching rebel during the early twentieth century) simply because they were women. Indeed, their primary concerns were not of a feminist nature but rather of a commitment to the centrality of the African-American freedom struggle. Their primary concern was the life-threatening plight of all Africana people, both men and women, at the hands of a racist system. To cast them in the feminist mold, which de-emphasizes their major concerns, is, in this writer's opinion, an abomination and an outright insult to the level of their struggle.

The problem is that too many Africanans have taken the theoretical framework of "feminism" and have tried to make it fit their particular circumstance. Rather than create their own paradigm, naming and defining themselves, some Africana women scholars, in particular, are persuaded by White feminists to adopt or to adapt to the white concept and terminology of feminism. The real benefit of the amalgamation of black feminism and white feminism goes to white feminists who can increase their power base by expanding their scope with the convenient consensus that sexism is their commonality and primary concern. They make a gender analysis of African-American life only to equate racism with sexism. Politically and ideologically for Africana women, such an adoption is misguided and simplistic. Most Africanans do not share the same ideology with traditional white feminists. True, the two may share strategies for ending sexual discrimination, but they are divided on the methodology to change the entire political system that would end racial discrimination and sexual exploitation. While the white feminist has not sacrificed her major concern, sexism, the "black feminist" has, in that she has yielded her primary concerns for racism and classism as secondary and tertiary issues. The modified terminology, "Black Feminism," is some black women's futile attempt to fit into the constructs of an established white female paradigm. At best, black feminism may relate to sexual discrimination outside the Africana community, but cannot claim to resolve the critical problems within the Africana community that are influenced by racism and classism. White feminist Bettina Aptheker accurately analyzes the problem:

> When we place women at the center of our thinking, we are going about the business of creating an historical and cultural matrix from which women may claim autonomy and independence over their own lives. For women of color, such autonomy cannot be achieved in conditions of racial oppression and cultural

genocide....In short, "feminist," in the modern sense, means the empowerment of women. For women of color, such an equality, such an empowerment, cannot take place unless the communities in which they live can successfully establish their own racial and cultural integrity. (Aptheker 13)

For many white women, Africana women exist for their purpose--a dramatization of oppression. As for their identity, they define themselves as the definitive woman. There is no need, for example, to name their studies "White" Women Studies. Moreover, while gender-specific discrimination is the key issue for Women's Studies, it unfortunately narrows the goals of Africana liberation and devalues the quality of Africana life. Thus, it neither identifies nor defines the primary issue for Africana women or other women of color. Therefore, it is crucial that Africana women engage in self-naming and self-definition, lest they fall into the trap of refining a critical ideology at the risk of surrendering the critical self.

Africana women might begin by naming and defining their unique movement Africana womanism. Womanism can be traced back to Sojourner's speech, which begins to develop and highlight Africana women's unique experience into a paradigm of Africana women. In refining this terminology into a theoretical framework and methodology, Africana Womanism, while it identifies the participation and the role of Africana women in the struggle it does not suggest that female subjugation is the most critical issue they face in their struggle for parity. Like the so-called black feminism, Africana Womanism acknowledges gender problems in society as a critical one that must be resolved; however, it views feminism, the suggested alternative to the problem, as a sort of inverted white patriarchy, with the white feminist now in command and on top. In other words, mainstream feminism is women's co-opting themselves into main-stream patriarchal values. According to Gordon:

The Movement fails to state clearly that the system is wrong; what it does communicate is that White women want to be a part of the system. They seek power, not change. (Gordon: 47)

The Africana womanist, on the other hand, perceives herself as the companion to the Africana man and works diligently toward continuing their established union in the struggle against racial oppression. Within the Africana culture, there is that intrinsic, organic equality that was necessary for survival of the Africana culture, in spite of the individual personal problems of female subjugation infiltrating the family structure by the white male cultural system. This issue must be addressed. However, the white male's privilege is not the personal problem of the Africana man or woman; rather it is a political problem of unchallenged gender chauvinism in the world. Critiquing Women's Studies, Aptheker concludes that:

> *Women's studies programs operate within a racist structure. Every department in every predominantly white institution is centered on the experience, history, politics, and culture of white men, usually of the elite. What is significant, however, is that women's studies, by its very reason for existence, implies a reordering of politics, a commitment to community, and an educational purpose which is inherently subversive of its institutional setting....Insofar as women's studies replicates a racial pattern in which white rule predominates, however, it violates its own principles of origin and purpose. More to the point: it makes impossible the creation of a feminist vision and politics (Aptheker, 13).*

Africanans have more critical and complex problems in their community, and the source of these problems lies in racial oppression. Moreover, the Africana woman acknowledges the problem of classism, too, likewise a reproachable element in American's capitalistic system. However, even there—in the plight of the middle-class Africana women--it becomes intertwined with racism. Given that both the Africana womanist and the black feminist treat these same critical issues and more, there must be something that makes them different, and that something is prioritizing on the part of the Africana woman. She realizes the critical need to prioritize the antagonistic forces as racism, classism, and sexism respectively. In the final analysis, Africana Womanism is connected to the tradition of being self-reliant and autonomous, working toward participation in Africana liberation.

Observe the importance of Africana identity in the scenario of Sojourner Truth for example. Before one can properly address her much-quoted query, one must, as she did, first address her color, for it was because of color that Sojourner Truth was initially hissed and jeered at for having the gall to presume that she should have a voice on the matter of any conflict between the men and the women and on the rights of the latter. Before Sojourner Truth could hope to address gender problems, she had to first overcome the problem of color for whites. Clearly, gender was not the salient issue for her. The need to reiterate "And Aren't I a Woman?" suggests Sojourner was insisting that she, too, possessed all the traits of a woman, notwithstanding her race and class, which the dominate culture used to exclude her from the community. Hence, the key issue for the Africana woman, as well as for the Africana man, is racism, with classism intertwined therein.

While the point is well taken that women of all ethnic orientations share the unfortunate commonality of female subjugation, it is naive, to say the least, to suggest that this kind of oppression should be the primary concern of all women, particularly women of color. When the black feminist buys the white terminology, she also buys its agenda. As Africana women share other forms of oppression that are not necessarily a part of the overall white women's experiences, their varied kinds of victimization need to be prioritized. Instead of alienating the Africana male sector from the struggle today, Africanans must call for a renegotiation of Africana male-female roles in society. In so doing, there must be a call to halt female subjugation once and for all, while continuing the crucial struggle for the liberation of Africana people the world over.

The notion of Africana women moving "from margin to center" of the feminist movement, as proposed by black feminist Bell Hooks (who does a very good job in documenting the revolutionary role of Africana women in the abolitionist struggle) is ludicrous. For how can Africana women hope to move from the peripheral to the center of a movement that, historically, did not have her on the agenda? Even during the resurgence of the women's liberation movement of the mid-1960s, the critical concerns of the Africana woman was not on the agenda. In spite of this factor, Hooks complains that contemporary black women do not join together for women's rights because they do not see womanhood as an important aspect of their identity. Further, Hooks complains that racist and sexist socialization has conditioned black women to devalue their femaleness and to regard race as their only relevant label of identity. In short, she surmises that black women were asked to deny a part of themselves, and they did. Clearly this position evokes some controversy, as it does not take into account the dynamics of the Africana woman's reluctance to embrace feminism.

This writer is reminded of an experience a colleague had observed: From so many feet away, her race was noticed; as she moved into close proximity, her class was detected; but it was not until she got in the door that her sex was known. Does that not suggest the need for prioritization? Hence for Sojourner Truth, as for all Africana women, the first and foremost issue remains race, with class and sex following closely. Granted, the Africana woman does have additional battles to fight, for as history has revealed, her peculiar predicament within the dominant culture is that of a tripartite victim of racism, classism, and sexism.

The prioritizing the kinds of relegation to which the Africana woman is subjected should be explored in a serious effort to recognize and to understand the existence of her total sense of oppression. What one really wants to do is to appreciate the triple plight of Africana women. Society must deal with all aspects of the Africana woman's oppression in order to better combat them. Moreover, as the problems of race and then class, are the key societal issues for people of color, they must be resolved first if there is any hope for human survival. It is impossible to conceive of any human being succumbing to absolute regression without an outright struggle against it.

Sojourner Truth demonstrated early on in the women's rights movement that the commonality is betwixt the Africanans of the South (both men and women) in their struggle for freedom and the women of the North. Clearly, the Africana woman had no exclusive claim on the struggle for equal rights apart from her male counterpart. Africana men and Africana women are and should be allies, struggling as they have since slavery for equal social, economic, and political rights as fellow human beings in the world. There is an inherent contradiction in the ideology of "black feminism" that should be reevaluated. A more compatible terminology and concept is "Africana Womanism." Indeed, this issue must be properly addressed if Women's Studies is to be truly respected and if a positive agenda for African Women's Studies is to be truly realized.

(Reprint from *The Western Journal of Black Studies*, Vol. 13, No. 4, Fall 1989, 185-9)

Endnotes

[1] The term "Africana" is used to mean people of Africana descent, for example, African American, African Caribbean, and Continental Africans. The author introduced the "Africana Womanism" concept at the National Council for Black Studies Conference, March 1988.

[2] Sojourner Truth, "And Aren't I A Woman" in *Cavalcade*, editors, Arthur P. Davis and Saunders Redding (Boston: Houghton Mifflin Company, 1971), pp. 80-81

3 Vivian Gordon, Black Women, Feminism, and Black Liberation: Which Way? (Chicago: Third World Press, 1987), p. viii.

[4] NOW Statement of Purpose (Adopted at the organizing conference in Washington, D.C., October 29, 1966).

[5] Hazel V. Carby, *Reconstruction Womanhood: The Emergence of the Afro-American Woman Novelist* (New York: Oxford University Press, 1987), p. 6.

[6] Bettina Aptheker, "'Strong is What We Make Each Other': Unlearning Racism within Women's Studies" (*Women's Studies Quarterly*, 9:4 Winter 1981), p. 13.

7 Hooks, Bell. *Feminist Theory: From Margin to Center*, Southend Press, 1984.

BIBLIOGRAPHY

Aptheker, Betinna. "'Strong Is What We Make Each Other': Unlearning Racism within Women's Studies." *Women's Studies Quarterly*, 9:4 (Winter); 1981.

Carby, Hazel V. *Reconstructing Womanhood: The Emergence of the Afro-American Women Novelist.* New York: Oxford University Press, 1987.

Gordon, Vivian. *Black Women, Feminist, and Black Liberation Which Way?* Chicago: Third World Press, 1987.

Hooks, Bell. *Feminist Theory: From Margin to Center.* Southend Press, 1984.

National Organization of Women, Statement of Purpose. Washington, D.C. 29, October 1966.

Truth, Sojourner. "And Aren't I a Woman." In *Cavalcade.* Edited by Arthur P. Davis and Saunders Redding. (eds.), Boston: Houghton Mifflin Company, 1976, pp. 80-81.

CHAPTER TWO

Nommo: Self-Naming, Self-Definition and the History of Africana Womanism

"Definitions belonged to the definers--not the defined."

MORRISON, *BELOVED*

Africana Womanism, emerged from the acknowledgment of a long-standing authentic agenda for that group of women of African descent who needed only to be properly named and officially defined according to their own unique historical and cultural matrix, one that would reflect the co-existence of a man and a woman in a concerted struggle for the survival of their entire family/community. The process by which this phenomenon, a concept I named and defined in the mid-eighties (then called "Black Womanism"), took shape, and the open acknowledgment of its pre-existence was articulated in a 1998 publication, several years after my 1992 presentation at the First International Conference on Women of Africa and the African Diaspora at the University of Nigeria-Nsukka:

> *For nearly a decade, I have been actively working on naming and defining, via identifying and refining an African-centered paradigm for women of African descent. In observing the traditional role, character, and activity of this collective group,*

identified by their common African ancestry, I concluded during the early stages of my research that the phenomenon I named and defined as Africana Womanism had long been in existence, dating back to the rich legacy of African womanhood. Therefore, I did not create the phenomenon in and of itself, but rather observed Africana women, documented our reality, and refined a paradigm relative to who we are, what we do, and what we believe in as a people. [Hudson-Weems, "Self-Naming" 449]

The activity surrounding Africana/Black Womanism itself commenced in the fall of 1985, when, during my first semester as a Ph.D. student at the University of Iowa, I challenged Black feminism. At that time I used the terminology "Black Womanism," which later evolved to the present terminology--Africana Womanism. From the research paper I wrote that semester, entitled "The Tripartite Plight of the Black Woman—Racism, Classism and Sexism—in *Our Nig, Their Eyes Were Watching God* and *The Color Purple*," I was motivated to set up a panel for the 13-16, March 1986 National Council for Black Studies (NCBS) Annual Conference in Boston. I presented a paper there entitled "Black Womanism versus Black Feminism--Racism First, Sexism Last: The Survival of the Black Race," wherein an obvious paradigm is outlined in the title itself. While many black women at the conference, including two established sociologists, Delores Aldridge, then president of the NCBS, and Vivian Gordon, author of the 1987bpublication *Black Women, Feminism and Black Liberation: Which Way?*, concurred with my thesis of prioritization; others insisted on the simultaneity of these obstacles—race, class, and gender respectively—in the lives of Black women.

For the three years standing, from 1985 to 1988, and even to my first publication in 1989 on the subject, I relentlessly spoke out on this crucial subject at national conferences, most notably at a panel entitled "The Tripartite Plight of Black Women" for the 24-28, June 1987 National Women's Studies Association Convention in Atlanta, Georgia. That fall, the challenge presented to my work on black women continued and was taken up on an Iowa City local television program, "The Silver Tongue," where I debated a senior doctoral student, who would complete her studies there in 1989, approximately a year after I did. Later that semester, I continued to challenge Black feminism in a paper presented at a 1987 University of Iowa Black Survival Conference: "Black Womanism versus Black Feminism: A Critical Issue for Human Survival." The seed for two subsequent presentations came from this work, with some revisions—work that was well received at the 7-9, April 1988 National Council for Black Studies and later at the 28-30, April 1988 African Heritage Studies Association Annual Conferences. In fact, some of my colleagues acknowledged that feminism/black feminism, for some reason or another, did not quite work for them, and they expressed their gratitude for this new distinction.

The following year, the fruition of this long continuous work culminated in two publications: One was "Cultural and Agenda Conflicts in Academia: Critical Issues for Africana Women's Studies" which was released in the 1989 Winter Issue of *The Western Journal of Black Studies.* The other was "The Tripartite Plight of African-American Women as Reflected in the Novels of Hurston and Walker" which was released in the December 1989 issue of *The Journal of Black Studies.* A call for new terminology for articulating the historical and cultural reality of women of African descent was issued forth in the first article:

> *Africana women might begin by naming and defining their unique movement "Africana Womanism." The concept of Womanism can be traced back to Sojourner's [1852] speech that began to develop and highlight Africana women's unique experience into a paradigm for Africana women. [Hudson-Weems, "Cultural and Agenda Conflicts" 187]*

This new terminology, coupled with a new paradigm, expressed discontent with other female-based constructs (e.g.: feminism, black feminism, and womanism) that had not clearly expressed an agenda for Africana women relative to the prioritizing of their triple plight. To be sure, this sense of prioritizing is clearly delineated in Sojourner Truth's self actualization oration "And Ain't I a Woman," where she was obligated to address the race factor first, then the class factor, before she could even begin to entertain the absurd notion of female subjugation, the gender factor.

Four years later, in 1993, the publication of the book on this topic, *Africana Womanism: Reclaiming Ourselves,* was released, despite the fact that several publishers initially expressed hesitancy in publishing the manuscript. Their reluctance was in no small part due to the controversial issues surrounding black women's rejection of "mainstream" feminist ideology, that is, its caustic beginnings and its inapplicability for women of African descent. Significantly, *Africana Womanism* was at the center of existing debates and at the forefront of a new, even bolder controversy in its radical pronouncement of the abandonment of feminist terminology in labeling black women. Describing my work in the biographical head-notes preceding my contributed article to their text, the editors of *Call and Response: The Riverside Anthology of the African American Literary Tradition* asserted the following:

> *Taking a strong position that black women should not pattern their liberation after Eurocentric feminism but after the historic and triumphant women of African descent, Hudson Weems has launched a new critical discourse in the Black Women's Literary Movement [Hill 1811]*

At the same time, those black women (black feminists) who continued to use the term feminism as a theoretical construct for their analysis received unnumbered support for their research. Aligning themselves with the acceptable framework of feminism was unquestionably one of the most reliably strategic means of becoming initiated into that established community, which rendered many perks, such as visibility, prodigious employment possibilities, and publications. Clearly, such a *reward system* has been influential in black feminists and black feminist critics' allegiance to and identification with dominant feminist ideologies. Moreover, it is my conjecture that many may very well have viewed their acceptance of Africana Womanism not only as risking their professional security, but as invalidating their years of research from the Black feminist perspective. This, indeed, is unfortunate, for instead they should have viewed "it as a natural evolutionary process of ideological growth and development" for the black women's movement from black feminism to Africana Womanism (Hudson-Weems, ". . . Entering the New Millennium" 36). In the final analysis, then, in an attempt to reshape the feminist/black feminist agenda to suit their needs by ignoring an existing practical, theoretical, and more compatible construct, these prominent black feminists, having been "appropriated and reshaped into a revised form of black feminism," often duplicate much of the work that has already been done in Africana Womanism, distinguishable only, for the most part, by misnaming (Hudson-Weems, "Africana Womanism: An Overview" 206).

Exemplifying this practice is black feminist Evelyn Brooks Higginbotham in "African-American Women's History and the Metalanguage of Race," published in 1992, approximately six years after the inception of many powerful debates and publications delineating the importance of self-naming and self-defining for black women, which encompasses formulating one's own name, agenda, and priorities as highlighted in Black Womanism/Africana Womanism. To be sure, Higgenbotham was well aware of the fact that race had not been properly factored into the burgeoning field of Women's Studies, and thus, she called for "Feminist scholars, especially those of African-American women's history, [to] accept the challenge to bring race more prominently into their analysis of power" (Higginbotham 3), a call issued several years earlier in the announcement of Africana Womanism. Black feminist bell hooks, who unrealistically urged black women to move from the peripheral to the center of the feminist movement, which was founded by white women and justifiably tailored to their particular needs, later incorporated many of the descriptors outlines in *Africana Womanism* in one of her mid-nineties publications. Moreover, Patricia Hill Collins, in a 1995 article, "What's in a Name? Womanism, Black Feminism, and Beyond," inaccurately asserts that "No term currently exists that adequately represents the substance of what diverse groups of black women alternately call womanism and black feminism" (Collins 17). The truth of the matter is that the so-called non-existent term to which Collins refers had already been articulated years before in *Africana Womanism*, which was, at the time of her article, in its third revised edition. As the term Africana Womanism had been in existence since the mid-eighties, it is clear that, along with the terminology, a well-defined paradigm was also established. Even Alice Walker's "womanism" pronouncments—literally a page and one-half—does little more than present a brief commentary on the shade differentiation between what Collins notes as "alternately call[ed] womanism and black feminism"— purple vs. lavender. (See Walker's introduction to her collection of essays entitled *In Search of Our Mother's Gardens*.) Restating in her own words what Africana Womanism had pronounced a decade earlier, but without any reference to *Africana Womanism* itself, Collins contends:

> *Several difficulties accompany[ing] the use of the term "black feminism" . . . involves the problem of balancing the genuine concerns of black women against continual pressures to absorb and recast such interests within white feminist frameworks. . . the emphasis on [of white feminist] themes such as personal identity, understanding "difference" . . . and the simplistic model of the political . . . "personal is political," that currently permeate North American white women's feminism in the academy can work to sap black feminism of its critical edge [15].*

More important than the way the Academy, in collusion with feminism, has effectively diluted the "critical [black feminist] edge" is the tacit consent that black feminism has given both to the Academy and white feminism through its short-sighted forfeiture of the highly political edge that Africana Womanism offers. Even as black feminism attempts to correct its myopic vision through its incorporation of the substance of Africana Womanism, it fails to admit (while it omits) Africana Womanism's essential and underlying foundation— *nommo*, its name.

Collins' own shift to what she incorrectly claims to be a more culturally/globally centered approach to theorizing black women's resistance to all oppression is even more pronounced in her tenth and most recent edition of *Black Feminist Thought* (2000). Here she vividly points to the confusion and dysfunctionality that the term Black feminism engenders: "whereas this edition remains centered on U.S. black women, it raises questions concerning African American women's positionality within a global black feminism" (xii). Obviously, this type of confusion and these types of questions with regard to Africana women within any type of feminism is directly and clearly addressed within the authentic agenda put forth by Africana Womanism. Conversely, scholarship like that expressed in Collins' black feminism finds itself in a socio linguistic and cultural maze. Sadly, Collins demonstrates, through her own language, confusion about what aspects of black feminism she sees as part of a global address/appendage--Africana Womanism's prioritizing race, class, and gender-based paradigm or white feminism's gender-based system. Collins' misnaming of black women's resistance and thought through supposed "renaming" or appropriation of a "black" additive to an already baggage-laden feminist center does much to belie her claims to "global black feminism" and most certainly supports Africana Womanism's long-standing argument concerning the inherent and fundamental contradiction in the concept of black feminism itself. Collins unwittingly turns a light of truth on her own flawed system of naming as she addresses the problem of terminology with regard to paradigms like Afrocentricity. She glaringly and perhaps unconsciously supports Africana Womanism's thesis about the importance of naming and the incongruent relationship between the theory and practice of black feminism and the Africana women it claims to represent. Thus, Collins' contends that "When the same language continues to be used, whereas the meaning attached to it changes . . . the term becomes too value laden to be useful" (Collins xi). Her assertion here, which she later contradicts, clearly echoes and appropriates the underlying premise for Africana Womanism without so much as citing the source - as scholars must ethically do. For example, in "Cultural and Agenda Conflicts in Academia: Critical Issues for Africana Women's Studies," I insisted that "When the Black feminist buys the White terminology, she also buys its agenda" (Hudson'Weems, "Cultural" 188). Collins contradicts her notion of a non-existing alternative terminology for black women in her earlier publication, "What's in a Name?," yet later acknowledges its existence in *Black Feminist Thought*, tenth edition, does, in fact, list alternative terminologies:

> *Rather than developing definitions and arguing over naming practices—for example, whether this thought should be called Black Feminism, Womanism, Afrocentric Feminism, Africana Womanism, and the like—a more useful approach lies in revisiting the reasons why black feminist thought exists at all.* [Collins 22]

Clearly, from this quotation, we see that she has missed the point. Obviously she does not comprehend the concept of *nommo*, or she would not have ended by proposing such a question in the first place. More relevant is the question of why Collins retains the term, "feminist" and refuses a more authentic one? This is the dilemma within which black feminism, through its dysfunctional association with gender and illogical disassociation from race, finds itself. Pointing to the relationship between terminology, Africana Womanism, and its potential for effecting political change, Afrocentric scholar Ama Mazama highlights Hudson-Weems' Africana Womanism in rendering particularly useful contributions to the Afrocentric discourse on African women and men. Hudson-Weems coined the term *Africana Womanism* in 1987 out of the realization of the total inadequacy of feminism and like theories (e.g., Black Feminism, African Womanism, or Womanism) to grasp the reality of African women, let alone give us the means to change that reality. [Mazama 400]

Notwithstanding the failure of black feminists to utilize Africana Womanism as a tool for analyzing Africana women's lives, and the way this original paradigm has affected our perception and fostered a deeper understanding of our agenda in the past twelve to fifteen years is evident. But the voice of Africana Womanism will not and cannot be silenced, and like the true Africana womanist, who has never really needed to "break silence" or to "find voice," the expressed sentiments of many feminists, I have continued—through my ever-evolving critical paradigm—to uphold the Africana womanist agenda and priorities within Africana historical and cultural contexts. Such contexts are reflected in our on going struggle for the human rights of our entire family—men, women, and children.

Using Africana Womanism as a spring board, Valethia Watkins, in "Womanism and Black Feminism: Issues in the Manipulation of African Historiography," interrogates Nancie Caraway's critique of the failure of white feminists to document black women's role in the feminist movement. While Caraway's critique appears a sincere gesture to "correct" the past regarding its omission of black women from the feminist arena, the Black Feminist Revisionist Project, a response to Caraway's work, was flawed at its inception for various reasons. To begin with, the very intent and design of the project to reclaim *all* black women as feminists, particularly activists in our on-going liberation struggle – e.g.: Sojourner Truth, Harriet Tubman, Anna Julia Cooper, Ida B. Wells, Rosa Parks--presupposes the primacy of a white history of resistance. Thus, the

Black Revisionist Project problematically locates black activism, dating back in antiquity, outside of its historical reality. In other words, naming black women activists after white women, black feminists, is in essence "duplicating a duplicate," since in reality, feminists often modeled their strategies after black activists models, such as antislavery abolitionism, the civil rights movements, and other political frameworks for survival that are found in black history and black communities (Hudson-Weems, *Africana Womanism* 22). In fact, they go so far as to claim any and all activities and perspectives related to (black) women as black feminist. One blatant example of this is in placing Toni Morrison's 1971 *New York Time Magazine* article "What the Black Woman Thinks about Women's Lib" in a 2000 feminist publication entitled *Radical Feminism*, edited by Barbara A. Crow, which, by its very inclusion in this feminist text of such a title, presumes or more significantly suggests that the article belongs to a feminist arena. In that article, Morrison is clearly not espousing a feminist agenda for female empowerment; rather she asserts that "the early image of Women's Lib was of an elitist organization made up of upper-middle class women with the concerns of class and not paying much attention to the problems of most black women" (Morrison, quoted. in *Radical Feminism*, 455). Moreover, in Wendy Harding and Jacky Martin's *A World of Difference: An Intercultural Study of Toni Morrison's Novels*, which was published in 1994, quoted Morrison as saying that she "feels to much emphasis is placed on gender politics," and hence her emphasis on the cruelties and horrific after effects of slavery are justified (Harding 61). If anything, her focus here is on race— i.e., on the exclusion of black women's concerns. And this is only one example of unconscionable acts in the academy.

Tragically, dating back to the inception of the Black Feminist Revisionist Project, black women scholars, according to this project's documentation, stood "silent" on mislabeling black women activists, thinkers, etc. as black feminists. Critiquing this practice, Watkins contends:

> *Despite the sheer magnitude and scope of the Black Feminist Revisionist Project, it has gone virtually unchallenged, and it has been met with silence, by and large, by the community of African-centered scholars. One notable exception to our complicity with*

this project, through our silence, has been a critical commentary written by Clenora Hudson-Weems . . . [who] contends that this revisionist process of inappropriately labeling African women is both arbitrary and capricious. Similarly, she argues that a feminist procrustean agenda de-emphasizes and recasts the primary concern of African women of the nineteenth and early twentieth century. According to Hudson-Weems, the primary concern of the women and men of this era was the life-threatening plight of African people, male and female. Black feminist revisionism changes this focus into a narrow feminist concern which prioritizes the plight of women as delinked and somehow different from the condition of the men in their community. [258]

Of course, refusal to surrender the authentic agenda for Africana women, notwithstanding the many personal and professional sacrifices, has paved the way for contemporary black women to follow, even though many, some them are cited above, have failed to acknowledge Africana Womanism as a legitimate paradigm and model. They have too often camouflaged their so called "new black feminism," as proposed by Hortense Spillers, wherein they can more equally deal with gender and race issues, suggesting that an adequate model of resistance against female oppression for black women in a racist society does not already exist within Africana cultures and society. With their revised theory, they position themselves straddling the fence and thus, remain ideologically acceptable by the dominant culture.

It should be here noted here that in the wake of more recognition of the cultural diversity that exists within the general population and by extension its concomitant global perspectives on gender, the dominance of mainstream gender perspectives is waning and Africana Womanism, at the center of the debate for well over a decade, is at the forefront of this transcultural revisitation of a woman's place in society. In addition to an interview that Kay Bonetti conducted in 1995 for *The American Audio Prose Library, Inc.* on *Africana Womanism,* many scholars have asked me for chapters, articles, or reprints of my work that deal with Africana Womanism for their publications. Thus, my work has been included in such publications as *Call and Response: The Riverside Anthology of the*

African American Literary Tradition (1997); *A Historiographical and Bibliographical Guide to the African American Experience* (2000); *Out of the Revolution: The Development of Africana Studies* (2000); *Sisterhood, Feminisms and Power* (1998); and *State of the Race, Creating Our 21ˢᵗ Century* (2003). Other book chapters will appear in *Black Studies: From the Pyramids and Pan Africanism and Beyond* (2002), and *Keepers of the Flame* (2003). In my edited book entitled *Contemporary Africana Theory and Thought* (2003), there is an entire section devoted to scholarship on the application of Africana Womanism. Additionally, I received and accepted an offer to be contributing editor for a special issue on *Africana Womanism* for the 2002 Spring Issue of *The Western Journal of Black Studies*, which includes several articles by Africana womanist scholars. Thus, Africana Womanism is indisputably creating a new wave for black women and the black women's movement in particular on all fronts.

Be that as it may, many were impressed with this new paradigm from the very beginning, and I received numerous invitations to speak at institutions across the nation, including an invitation from Winston-Salem State University's 1988 Black History Month Program, where I had the occasion to meet and converse with renowned scholar, the late Dr. C. Eric Lincoln, Professor Emeritus of Duke University, who endorsed *Africana Womanism: Reclaiming Ourselves.*

> *Hudson-Weems's Africana Womanism sent unaccustomed shock waves through the domain of popular thinking about feminism, and established her as a careful, independent thinker, unafraid to unsettle settled opinion.* [Lincoln quoted in *Africana Womanism*]

Demands for colloquy on this controversial topic grew, complimented by invited speaking engagements - sometimes as many as fifteen a year on this subject alone--at such national/international colleges and universities as the University of Nigeria-Nsukka, University of Utah, Bryn Mawr College, Mary Washington University, Cornell University, Texas Southern University, Illinois Wesleyan University, University of Rhode Island, Central State University, University of Michigan-Flint, University of Illinois-Springfield, LeMoyne-Owen College, Northern Illinois University, Kean University, Drew University, California State

University-Long Beach, Virginia Commonwealth University, Wayne State University, Stillman College, Southern Utah State University, Kentucky State University, University of Wisconsin-Milwaukee, Temple University, University of the West Indies-Barbados, and the University of Gwelph (Canada). In addition to numerous invitations as guest speaker at institutions of higher learning, I have also been the keynote, plenary, round-table, banquet and luncheon speaker at national/international conventions, among them the National Council for Black Studies Annual Conference, the African Heritage Studies Association Annual Conference, the Annual Meeting of The Association for the Study of African American Life and History, College Language Association Annual Conference, the International Conference on Women of Africa and the African Diaspora, Chicago State University's Black Writers' Annual Conference, the Annual Third World Conference, the National Conference on Civil/Human Rights of Africananas, the Annual Diop International Conference, and the U.S. Army Ft. Leonard Wood Black History Month Luncheon (keynote address). Finally, faculty in several institutions of higher learning in far away places like England, South Africa, Germany, Nigeria Brazil, Japan, the Caribbean Islands, utilize *Africana Womanism*. National universities also utilize it, among them California State University-Long Beach, University of North Texas, Florida A & M University, Western Michigan University, Indiana State University, Northern Illinois University, San Francisco State University, Temple University, the University of Arizona, the University of Michigan-Flint, the University of Missouri-Columbia, and the University of Utah to name a few.

Having presented the history of the emergence, evolution, and subsequent dominance of Africana Womanism, I will now turn to a brief history of the critical acceptance of Africana Womanism within cultural and literary studies, focusing on the relationship of these endorsements to the specific agenda. The Editors of *Call and Response: The Riverside Anthology of the African American Literary Tradition* credited me as the "first African American woman intellectual to formulate a position on Africana Womanism [in her] groundbreaking study *Africana Womanism: Reclaiming Ourselves*" (Hill 1811).

In the foreword to *Africana Womanism*, the late 'Zula Sofola, the internationally renown scholar revered as Nigeria's first female playwright, describes the work as "not simply a scholarly work, one of those in the mainstream, but our own. It is a new trail blazed with incontrovertible revelations on the African heritage and gender question. Hudson-Weems bravely takes the bull by the horns, confronts the Eurocentric avalanche of works on questions of gender, and puts forward the Afrocentric point of view" [Quoted in *Africana Womanism* xvii].

Daphne Ntiri-Queman, the Sierra Leonean scholar recognized as an expert on women's issues, spent years as a delegate to the United Nations and consultant to Senegal, Kismayo, and Somalia under the auspices of UNESCO, and in her Introduction to *Africana Womanism* she insists:

> *This landmark pioneering treatise of Africana woman's realities cannot be ignored. . . . It will unlock closed doors and usher in a spirit of renewed plentitude. Africana Womanism is reminiscent of a comparable avant garde movement of the 1930s by diasporan [sic] Black scholars Leopold Sedar Senghor, Leon Damas, and Aime Cesaire, who struggled to seek reassurance of their blackness. [Quoted in Africana Womanism 10-11]*

In "The WAAD Conference and Beyond: A Look at Africana Womanism," in *Sisterhood, Feminisms and Power: From Africa to the Diaspora*, Ntiri Queman contends that "Its [Africana Womanism's] purpose is multifunctional as it serves as the conceptual tool which harnesses the transformative energies and strategies embedded in Africana women's rise from oppression" (Ntiri 462). Later in "Africana Womanism: Coming of Age" in [*Contemporary Africana Theory and Thought*], she concludes:

> *Just as there are compelling reasons to reclaim the power to ascribe names to African people (e.g., colored, Negro, African, African-American) in the United States (to reaffirm their race and establish stronger African affinity), so are there reasons to advocate an Africana womanist theory that is properly labeled, more attuned, and appropriate to the needs of the Africana woman*

Delores Aldridge, holder of an Endowed Chair in Sociology and Africana American Studies at Emory University, endorsed the book in 1993 as "unquestionably a pioneering effort whose time has come." In her edited book, *Out of the Revolution: The Development of Africana Studies*, in which I have contributed a chapter, her chapter "Towards Integrating Africana Women into Africana Studies," presents her juxtaposition of Black women's activities and Africana Studies with Women's Studies. Here she discusses the history of the caustic beginnings of feminism as presented in *Africana Womanism*, which cites Carrie Capman Catt's contention that white men must recognize "the usefulness of woman suffrage as a counterbalance to the foreign vote, and as a means of legally preserving white supremacy in the South" (quoted in Hudson-Weems, *Africana Womanism*, 21). Aldridge concludes, "it is from this perspective of Africana Womanism that this discourse [on integrating Africana women in Africana Studies] is developed" (Aldridge 193). She also refers to my thesis on Africana Womanism as a "revolutionary work [that] has no parallel as a new way of understanding Africana women" (196). Finally, in her forthcoming article "Black Male-Female Relationships: An African Centered Lens Model" in the book *Contemporary Africana Theory and Thought*, she adds me to her "chorus of voices [that] have criticize [d] feminism (LaRue, 1970, Duberman, 1975, Gordon, 1987, [and] Hudson-Weems, 1989 and 1993)."

Talmadge Anderson Professor Emeritus at Washington State University, and Founding Editor for *The Western Journal of Black Studies*, concludes in his book endorsement that the "work captures the essence of the true meaning of Black womanhood and resolves the classical debate relative to the prioritizing of race, class and sex in American society." Similarly, Robert Harris, vice provost and former director of the Africana Studies and Research Center at Cornell University, asserts the following:

In the triple marginality of Black women, race rises above class and gender in this remarkable book. With it, a reunion, a much needed healing, a human philosophy emerges for men and women of African ancestry and ultimately for all caring men and women. [Quoted. in Africana Womanism]

The late Maria Mootry, Respected literary critic, original Black Bio-ethicist, and author of the seminal work in this area, "Confronting Racialized Bioethics: New Contract on Black America" (*Western Journal of Black Studies* 2000), taken from her unpublished manuscript *Brain Games: Race, Bioethics and the Seduction of the American Mind*, stated the following in her review of *Africana Womanism*:

> *Now comes a voice, cool and clear, rising above the chorus, offering not only lucid insights into the status of Africana women and their literature, but a blueprint to help us find a way out of confusion and despair. In Africana Womanism: Reclaiming Ourselves, in its second revised edition after only seven months, Clenora Hudson-Weems examines the perceptions women in the African diaspora have of their historical and contemporary roles. She treads fearlessly through the maze of tension between mainstream feminism, Black feminism, African feminism, and Africana Womanism. The result, in the words of Professor Charles Hamilton, is "an intellectual triumph." [244]*

Daisy Lafond, former editor of *Voice: The Caribbean International Magazine*, writes the following in *Class Magazine*:

> *Molefe Kete Asante gave us Afrocentricity, to help us relocate ourselves from the margins of European experiences to the centrality of our own. Now, Clenora Hudson-Weems, in her second book Africana Womanism: Reclaiming Ourselves, is helping black women relocate themselves from the margins of white feminism to the centrality of their own experiences [Lafond 57].*

Finally, April Langley proclaims, in "Lucy Terry Prince: The Cultural and Literary Legacy of Africana Womanism," in *The Western Journal of Black Studies*, that

> *It is Africana Womanism as originated, developed, and outlined by Hudson-Weems that enables a reading which restores and revises the African origins of the earlier African American*

> *writing. . . . the import of this critical paradigm for the earliest*
> *Africana writers is essential for recuperating what is "African"*
> *in early African American literature. [Langley 158]*

Other scholars who view Africana Womanism as a viable concept include P. Jane Splawn ("Recent Developments in Black Feminist Literary Scholarship: A Selective Annotated Bibliography?" in *Modern Fiction Studies*, 1993;, Philip L. Kilbride ("Africana Womanism" in *Plural Marriages for Our Times: A Reinvented Option?*, 1994); Mary Ebun Modupe Kolawole (*Womanism and African Consciousness*, 1997); Tolagbe Ogunleye, aka: Dr. Martin Ainsi ("African Women and the Grassroots: The Silent Partners of the Women's Movement" in *Sisterhood, Feminisms, and Power: From Africa to the Diaspora*, 1998); Robson Delany, (Ninteenth-Century Africana Womanist: Reflections on His Avant-Garde Politics Concerning Gender, Colorism, and Nation Building" in *The Journal of Black Studies*, 1998); Olabisi Regina Jennings ["Why I Joined the Black Panther Party: An Africana Womanist Reflection" in *The Black Panther Party Reconsidered*, 1998, "Africana Womanism in the Black Panther Party: A Person Story" in *The Western Journal of Black Studies*, 2002 and "Africana Womanist Interpretation of Gwendolyn Brooks' in *Maud Martha*, 2002]; (First International Conference on Women in Africa and the African Diaspora: A View from the USA" in *Sisterhood*, 1998); Janette Y. Taylor ("Womanism: A Methodologic Framework for African American Women" in *Advances in Nursing Science*, 1998); P. S. Brush ("The Influence of Social-Movements on Articulations of Race and Gender in Black Women's Autobiography" in *Gender and Society*, 1999); Yolanda Hood ("Africana Womanism and Black Feminism: Re-reading African Women's Quilting Traditions," AFS Annual Meeting, 1999); Laverne Gyant ("The Missing Link: Women in Black/Africana Studies" in *Out of the Revolution: The Development of Africana Studies*, 2000); Carolyn Kumah ("African Women and Literature" in *West Africa Review*, 2000); Deborah Plant ("African Gender Trouble and Africana Womanism: An Interview with Chikwenye Ogunyemi and Wanjira Muthoni" in *Signs*, 2000); JoAnne Banks Wallace ("Womanist Ways of Knowing: Theoretical Considerations for Research with African American Woman" in *Advances in Nursing Science*, 2000); Madhu Kishwar ("Feminism, Rebellious Women and Cultural Boundaries:

Re-reading Flora Nwapa and Her Compatriots," 2001); Ama Mazama ("The Afrocentric Paradigm: Contours and Definitions" in *The Journal of Black Studies*, 2001); Adele Newson-Horst ("Gloria Naylor's *Mama Day*: An Africana Womanist Reading" in *Contemporary Africana Theory and Thought*, 2003); ("Maud Martha Brown: A Study in Emergence" in *Maud Martha: A Critical Collection*, 2002); Pamela Yaa Assantewaa Reed ("*Africana Womanism* and *African Feminism*: A Dialectic" in *The Western Journal of Black Studies*, 2001); Anne Steiner ("Frances Watkins Harper: Eminent Pre-Africana Womanist" in *Contemporary Africana Theory and Thought*, 2003); Betty Taylor Thompson [("Common Bonds from the U.S. to Africa and Beyond: Africana Womanist Literary Analysis" in *The Western Journal of Black Studies*, 2001) and (*Contemporary Africana Theory and Thought*, 2003)]; Antonio Tillis (*Hispanic Journal*, "Nancy Morejon's Mujer Negra" An Africana Womanist Reading" in 2001), Barbara Wheeler ("Africana Womanism: An African Legacy--It Ain't Easy Being a Queen" in *Contemporary Africana Theory and Thought*, 2002). Theoretical constructs that have been influenced by Africana Womanism include Kawaida Womanism, emerging from Maulana Karenga's Kawieda, and Afrocentric Womanism, coming out of the school of Afrocentricity as popularized by Molefe Asante.

Even those who have either consciously or unconsciously appropriated Africana Womanism demonstrate the overarching presence and validity of this concept. Notably, we have among many Tuzyline Jita Allan (*Womanist and Feminist Aesthetics*); Doris M. Boutain ("Critical Nursing Scholarship: Exploring Critical Social Theory with African American Studies" in *Advances in Nursing Science*, 1999); Michelle Collison ("Race Women Stepping Forward" in *Black Issues in Higher Education* 1999); Nah Dove ("African Womanism: An Afrocentric Theory" in *Sage*, 1998); Lynnett Harvey (*Why Black Women Reject Feminism: Racism in the Feminist Movement*, 1997); Anthonia Kalu ("Women in African Literature" *African Transitions* 2000); and Gail M. Presby ("Culture, Multiculturalism, and Intercultural Philosophy" in *Forum for Intellectual Philosophizing*, 2000).

Considering the history, the acceptance, and the pronounced demand for its dynamic critical framework, I have been challenged to re-articulate and to further develop the critical principles of Africana Womanism. Since Africana people have long been denied not only the authority of naming self, but, moreover, of defining self (as inferred by the narrator of Nobel prize-winning author, Toni Morrison's *Beloved* –"Definitions belonged to the definers--not the defined") it is now of utmost importance that we take control over both these determining interconnected factors in our lives if we hope to avoid degradation, isolation, and annihilation in a world of greed, violence and pandemonium (190). Self-namer and self-definer, two of the eighteen characteristics of the Africana woman, are seminal descriptors that delineate the first step in establishing an authentic paradigm relative to the true level of struggle for women of African descent, as this gets to the very crux of the matter and the history of Africana Womanism. From the authentic act of self-naming and self-defining, this critical paradigm emerged. At its very core/center lies *nommo*, an African term that cultural theorist, Molefi Kete Asante, calls "the generative and productive power of the spoken word" (Asante 17). It is a powerful and useful concept holding that the proper naming of a thing will in turn give it essence. Particularizing and advancing the concept, Harrison contends that "Nommo, in the power of the word . . . activates all forces from their frozen state in a manner that establishes concreteness of experience . . . be they glad or sad, work or play, pleasure or pain, in a way that preserves [one's] humanity" (Harrison xx). In African cosmology, the word *nommo*, then, evokes material manifestation. Thus, as Barbara Christian summarizes, "It is through nommo, the correct naming of a thing, that it comes into existence" (157-158), a profound statement to which she herself fails to adhere in calling herself a black feminist. While initiating a call for proper naming, I also insisted on our own agenda and our particular priorities of race, class, and gender respectively, contrary to the feminists' female-centered agenda with female empowerment as their number one priority. The other descriptors outlined in *Africana Womanism* are family-centered (in concert with the men in the liberation struggle), strong, genuine in sisterhood, whole, authentic, respected, recognized, male compatible, flexible role player, adaptable, respectful of elders, spiritual, ambitious, mothering, and nurturing.

The long-standing focus on the woman and her role in the greater society continues to be at the center of controversy today. For over a century and a half, dating back to pre-Civil War/Emancipation Proclamation, women have been engaged in shaping their role within the context of a particular social reality, one in which white males predominate within a racist patriarchal system. Although racism is clearly a seminal component of the overall system of oppression, white women in general, and the feminist movement in particular, have both been driven almost exclusively by issues related solely to gender oppression. However, the vast majority of black women have necessarily focused their energies on combating racism first before addressing the gender question. As a consequence, it is clear that the two groups ultimately have disparate goals for meeting their specific needs. In short, for black women, who are family-centered, it is race empowerment; for white women, who are female-centered, it is female empowerment. Because of this difference in agendas, distinct naming, then, is critical.

Noted black psychologist Julia Hare makes a profound comment on the reality of the difference in the politics of black life and that of white life, particularly in terms of the difference in certain meanings and ideals relative to the two parallel groups.

> *Women who are calling themselves black feminists need another word that describes what their concerns are. Black feminism in not a word that describes the plight of black women. In fact, . . . black feminists have not even come together and come to a true core definition of what black feminism is. The white race has a woman problem because the women were oppressed. Black people have a man and woman problem because Black men are as oppressed as their women. [Quoted in Phillip, 15]*

Hare's 1993 call for another name for the black woman's movement, because of the problematic dynamics of the terminology black feminism, offers insights into the significance of self-naming, and by extension self-definition, for the integrity and survival of Africana people. While her call indicates that she was unaware of the existence of the term Africana Womanism as a paradigm for all women of African descent, dating back to the eighties, her seminal statement, nonetheless, echoes the underlying concept of Africana Womanism in the on-going undercurrent debate both within and beyond the Academy surrounding the politics of black and white life. What is particularly disturbing here is the dominant culture's failure to acknowledge proper names, identifications, and systems even when they do exist, as is the case of Africana Womanism. Rather, the dominant culture too often promotes distortions of black life and models, the one constancy in an ever-changing climate of dissension and confusion revolving around the lives and destinies of black women and their families. Commanding different terminologies to reflect different meanings, this proper self-naming and self-defining, as a means of establishing clarity, will at the same time offer the first steps towards correcting confusion and misconception regarding one's true identity and the true level of one's struggle in terms of agenda. Hare's statement, then, reflects the nuances of the relativity of a particular terminology and concept--feminism—as issued forth by whites, and its inapplicability to black women as well as their male counterparts who are trapped first and foremost by the race factor rather than by the gender factor so prevalently addressed today. Hence, it is the crucial need for self-naming and self-defining, an interconnecting phenomenon that becomes penultimate as we come to understand truly that *giving name to* a particular thing simultaneously gives it meaning.

Because of the critical race factor for blacks, another scholar, Audrey Thomas McCluskey, insists that "Black women must adopt a culturally specific term to describe their racialized experience, " as she is astutely cognizant of that reality for black women, whether or not black women on the whole pursue this issue to the point of independently naming themselves. McCluskey contends, "the debate over names reflects deeper issues of the right to self-validation and to claim intellectual traditions of their own" (McCluskey 2). Another scholar, Linda Anderson Smith, also writes about the importance of naming. In her article, "Unique Names and Naming Practices among African American Families," she asserts:

> *Names are universally recognized as having power—as evoking images or signifying membership in a particular collective. Names are of great significance to African Americans, who, because of the history of slavery, have had to fight for the right to choose their names" [Smith 290].*

Ben L. Martin, too, notes the importance of naming in "From Negro to Black to African American: The Power of Names and Naming," where he states that "names can be more than tags; they can convey powerful imagery. So naming–proposing, imposing, and accepting names–can be a political exercise" (Martin 83).

While this process seems to be a natural course of action, society, on the contrary, has not taken this route. Rather, it has ignored the true operational existence of this long-standing phenomenon and has elected to name and define Africana women outside of their cultural and historical context via the superimposition of an alien construct–Eurocentrism/feminism. In essence, the dominant culture has held the position of identifying who we are and how we fit into the scheme of things with little regard for what we ourselves perceive as our authentic reality and identity. Instead of respecting our lives as representative of self-authentication, the dominant culture obtrudes itself upon Africana people. Pointing to Africana Womanism as a successful strategy and corrective for this obtrusion, Mazama asserts that "the term Africana Womanism itself is the first step toward defining ourselves and setting goals that are consistent with our culture and history. In other words, it is the first step toward existing on our own terms" (Mazama 400-401). It must be noted here that "it is true that if you do not name and define yourself, some else surely will" (Hudson-Weems, "Africana Womanism and the Critical Need" 83). And they usually do so miserably. Thus, in the midst of this legacy of continued European domination through improper identification, Africana people must actively reclaim their identity, beginning with self-naming and self-defining. To be sure, without reinventing pre-existing wheels, we could then move more expediently towards resolving the problems of human survival through family cohesiveness, which Africana Womanism most certainly offers.

(Reprint, Chapter 18, *Contemporary Africana Theory, Thought & Action*, 2007)

BIBLIOGRAPHY

Aldridge, Delores. "Black Male-Female Relationships: An African Centered Lens Model." In *Contemporary Africana Theory and Thought and Action: A Guide to Africana Studies.* Edited by Clenora Hudson-Weems. Trenton, New Jersey: Africa World Press, 2003.

_____"The Structural Components of Violence in Black Male-Female Relationships." *Journalof Human Behavior in the Social Environment* Vol. 4, No. 2 & 3, (2001); 13-24.

_____"Towards Integrating Africana Women into Africana Studies." In *Out of the Revolution:The Development of Africana Studies.* Edited by Delores Aldridge and Charlene Young. Lanham/New York: Lexington Books, 2000, pp 191-203.

Asante, Molefi Kete. *The Afrocentric Idea.* Philadelphia: Temple University Press, 1987.

Collins, Patricia Hill. "What's in a Name? Womanism, Black Feminism, and Beyond." *The Black Scholar* 26, 1 (Winter/Spring 1996): 921.

_____*Black Feminist Thought: Knowledge, Consciousness and the Politics of Empowerment.*10ᵗʰ Anniversary, 2ⁿᵈ ed. rev. New York: Routledge, 2000.

Harding, Wendy and Jacky Martin. *A World of Differences: An Intercultural Study of Toni Morrison's Novels.* London: Greenwood Press, 1994.

Hare, Julia. "Feminism in Black and White." Quoted in *Black Issues in Higher Education,* by Mary-Christine Phillip. 11, March 1993, pp. 12-17

Harrison, Paul Carter. *The Drama of Nommo.* New York: Grove Press, 1972.

Higginbotham, Everly Brooks. "African-American Women's History and the Metalanguage of Race." *Signs: Journal of Women in Culture and Society* 17, 2 (Winter 1992). 251-275.

Hill, Patricia Liggins. *Call and Response: The Riverside Anthology of the African American Literary Tradition.* Boston/New York: Houghton Mifflin, 1998.

Hudson-Weems, Clenora. "Africana Womanism: An Overview." In *Out of the Revolution: The Development of Africana Studies.* Edited by Delores Aldridge and Charlene Young. Lanham/New York: Lexington Books, 2000, 205-217.

_____"Africana Womanism and the Critical Need for Africana Theory and Thought." *The Western Journal of Black Studies* 21, 2 (1997); 79-84.

_____"Africana Womanism: Entering the New Millennium." In *State of the Race: Creating Our 21st Century: Where Do We Go from Here?* Kamara, Jemadari, and Van Der Meer, T. Menelik ed. Boston: University of Massachusetts Press, 2002, 1-45.

_____*Africana Womanism: Reclaiming Ourselves.* Troy, Mich: Bedford Publisher, 1993.

_____*Africana Womanism: Reclaiming Ourselves.* 3rd rev. ed. Michigan: Bedford Publishers, 1995.

_____"Cultural and Agenda Conflicts in Academia: Critical Issues for Africana Women's Studies." *The Western Journal of Black Studies*, 13, 4 (1988); 185-189.

Langley, April. "Lucy Terry Prince: The Cultural and Literary Legacy of Africana Womanism." In *The Western Journal of Black Studies*, Fall 2001.

Martin, Ben L. "From Negro to Black to African American: The Power of Names and Naming." *Political Science Quarterly* 106, 1 (Spring 1991): 83-107.

Mazama, Ama. "The Afrocentric Paradigm: Contours and Definitions." *Journal of Black Studies* 31, 4 (2001). 387-405.

McCluskey, Audry Thomas. "Am I Not a Woman and a Sister?: Reflections on the Role of Black Women's Studies in the Academy." *Feminist Teacher* 8, 3 (1994): 105-111.

Mootry, Maria K. "Book Review of *Africana Womanism: Reclaiming Ourselves*" in *The Western Journal of Black Studies* 18, 4 (1994).

Morrison, Toni. *Beloved.* New York: Alfred A. Knopf, 1987

_____"What the Black Woman Thinks about Women's Lib." In *Radical Feminism: A Documentary Reader.* Edited by Barbara A. Crow. New York: New York University Press, 2000.

Ntiri, Daphne. "The WAAD Conference and Beyond: A Look at Africana Womanism." In *Sisterhood, Feminisms and Power: From Africa to the Diaspora.* Edited by Obioma Nnaemeka. Trenton: Africa World Press, 1998, 461-463.

_____Introduction to *Africana Womanism: Reclaiming Ourselves.* Troy, Mich: Bedford Publishers, 1993, 1-13.

_____"Africana Womanism: The Coming of Age." In *Contemporary Africana Theory and Thought and Action.* Edited by Clenora Hudson-Weems. Trenton, New Jersey: Africa World Press, 2002.

Smith, Linda Anderson. "Unique Names and Naming Practices Among African American Families." *Families in Society* 77, 5 (May 1996): 290-298.

Sofola, 'Zulu. Foreword to *Africana Womanism: Reclaiming Ourselves.* Troy, MI: Bedford Publishers.

Watkins, Valethia. "Womanism and Black Feminism: Issues in the Manipulation of African Historiography." In *The Preliminary Challenge.* Los Angeles, Calif.: Association for the Study of Classical African Civilization, 1997.

CHAPTER THREE

The 18 Descriptors of the Africana Womanist

The fact of the matter is that Africana Womanism is a response to the need for collective definition and the re-creation of the authentic agenda that is the birthright of every living person.

(ASANTE, AFTERWORD, AFRICANA WOMANIST, 138)

It is the responsibility of Africana women to name and define themselves as implied in the above quotation and this chapter attempts to do just that, lest we fall victim to being misnamed and ill-defined by others. There are many positive characteristics of a true Africana womanist, but there are eighteen (18) distinct features as I have observed them time and again as accurately describing her nature and actions for centuries, dating back to antiquity. They are self-namer, self-definer, family centered, genuine in sisterhood, strong, in concert with male in struggle, whole, authentic, flexible role player, respected, recognized, spiritual, male compatible, respectful of elders, adaptable, ambitious and mother and nurturing.

As the old saying goes, there is nothing new in the universe. Well, that is true also of the Africana woman, as modern day Africana women continue, though oftentimes unconsciously, the rich legacy of African womanhood. In her article, entitled "Africana Womanism—An African Legacy: It Ain't Easy Being a Queen," anthropologist, Dr. Barbara Wheeler, *make[s] some observations about the world-wide institutions of marriage and family. The conclusion contains thoughts regarding the visible legacy of ancient African queens, queen warriors, and ordinary African women, and their impact upon contemporary women of African heritage. . . .*

It has now been acknowledged that humankind originated in Africa; that is, that the continent of Africa is the cradle of humanity. We also know that the hand that rocks the cradle historically has been the hand of a woman, the culture bearer. It is for this reason that we must laud Lewis, Mary, and Richard Leakey for resurrecting the oldest known African queen. In 1962, from the diggings of Olduvai Gorge, in Tanzania, the Leakeys unearthed the fossil that helped establish that humans, as we know them today, did originate in Africa (Contemporary Africana Theory, 320 and 321).

That said, I will now define the eighteen descriptors listed above for the Africana womanist, which she embodies to a varying degree:

Self-Namer

Nommo, a term used in African cosmology to indicate naming, is critical. In fact, Barbara Christian, a major literary critic in the field of Africana literature, asserts that "it is through nommo, the correct naming of a thing that it comes into existence" (Christian, pp. 157-158). The Africana woman, in realizing and properly accessing herself and her movement, must, then, properly name herself and her movement, Africana womanist and Africana Womanism respectively. This is a key step, which many women of African descent have failed to address. While they have taken the initiative to differentiate their struggle from the White woman's struggle to some degree, they have yet to give their struggle its own name. For example, Filomina Chioma Steady, a well-known Africana critic, in her introduction to *The Black Woman Cross-Culturally* presents her case for an African feminism, which she calls "a less antagonistic brand of feminism" for Black women (23). She fails to see the problem of naming the movement of Africana women after the White feminist movement, thereby creating complexities in the Africana movement that would not otherwise exist. Although Steady erroneously calls the African woman "the original feminist," her analysis, in which she identifies the historical and current role and activity of the Africana woman, is very accurate:

> *True feminism springs from an actual experience of oppression, a lack of the socially prescribed means of ensuring one's well-being, and a true lack of access to resources for survival. True feminism is the reaction which leads to the development of greater resourcefulness for survival and greater self-reliance. Above all, true feminism is impossible without intensive involvement in production. All over the African Diaspora, but particularly on the continent, the black woman's role in this regard is paramount. It can, therefore, be stated with much justification that the black woman is to a large extent the original feminist. (36)*

To be sure, all that the Africana woman is and has been does not make her a feminist, which is a concept that evolved long after her beginnings in Africa. She is her own person, operating according to the forces in her life, and thus, her name must reflect the authenticity of her activity, not that of another culture.

Always a self-namer, even during American slavery when the White slave owners of the slave woman labeled her as a breeder for American society, the Africana womanist insisted on identifying herself as mother and companion. Even though her children and her spouse were often taken from her, a common slave phenomenon, she did not relinquish her identity, and thus, a grieving mother and companion, she often held to the memories of her family. She knew that regardless of how the dominant culture viewed her, her "humanness" (even though it was denied her in a technical sense) contradicted their naming of her. Hence, as Sojourner asserts, "I have born'd five children and seen 'em mos' all sold off into slavery, and when I cried out with mother's grief, none but Jesus heard and ain't I a woman?" (Truth, 104). In spite of all, she was a woman and a mother, not mere property, and no matter what, her White owners could neither control nor dictate her knowledge of these factors or her human response to them.

Self-Definer

Defining herself and her reality, the Africana womanist is, indeed, a self-definer. From an historical perspective, the Africana woman has always managed to eke out a separate, private reality for herself and her family, regardless of the fact that she has been ill-defined others, such as the slave master who sees and defines her as a breeder for the benefit of his personal resources. A close look at John Blassingame's *The Slave Community* reveals much evidence that the slaves, women included, as Africana women's activities have always been by and large collective, defined themselves and their community in terms of their African cultural experiences, retaining the African ways in African-American culture. According to Christian, there is:

> *a persistent and major theme throughout Afro-American women's literature—our attempts to define and express our totality rather than being defined by others. (159)*

White feminist Sharon Welch admits "I cannot speak for African-American women or offer a definitive interpretation of the moral tradition expressed in their lives and in their writings" (16). Thus the Africana womanist defines her own reality, with no particular allegiance to existing ideals. Cultural identity supersedes self-definition for the true Africana womanist.

Family-Centered

A chief feature of the Africana womanist is her family-centrality, as she is more concerned with her entire family rather than with just herself and her sisters. According to Zula Sofola, Nigeria's first female playwright:

> *The world view of the African is rooted in the philosophy of holistic harmony and communalism rather than in the individualistic isolationism of Europe. The principle of relatedness is the sine qua non of African social reality.[1]*

While the concern for the survival of her family, both personal and collective, are of utmost importance to the Africana womanist, the mainstream feminist is self-centered or female-centered, interested in self-realization and personal gratification. On this same note, Acholonu contends that:

> *feminism in this regard subscribes to exclusive individualism, which is a philosophy of life alien to Africans and therefore quite antithetical to our communal way of life.*[2]

The most conservative feminist seeks to replicate the individualism of White patriarchal capitalism, a self-centered phenomenon that threatens the very fabric of Africana life and culture. While the eradication of female subjugation on all levels of society is a critical problem for women in general, the problem of liberating an entire people—exploited, repressed, and oppressed solely on the basis of their race—is an even greater one. The Africana womanist does not have the luxury of centering her interests around herself as victim in society when the victimization of her entire community is at stake. She realizes that her individual safety and survival are strongly affected by the overall status of her community. Until her entire people are free, she is not free. Her struggle is directly intertwined with that of her people. Even if she does overcome the battle of sexism through a collective struggle of all women, she will still be left with the battle of racism facing both her family and herself.

From a historical perspective, Blassingame comments on the primacy of family for slaves in *The Slave Community*: "The family, while it had no legal existence in slavery, was in actuality one of the most important survival mechanisms for the slave" (151). Also coming from a historical perspective, John Hope Franklin and Alfred Moss in *From Slavery to Freedom* give a sound explanation of why Africana people place a high priority on family, highlighting the:

> *remarkable stability and resiliency of the black family ... their efforts to reunite and, in many instances, their taking steps to make their marriages and children legitimate after years and decades of living together as slaves with no marriage contract.* (208)

With such efforts to just stay together, the notion of the primacy of family cannot be overlooked. According to Leland Hall in "Support Systems and Coping Patterns," "The family is where the Black male obtains his initial exposure to an environment of support, love and affection" (161).

Because of the circumstance of the Africana community, in that American slavery necessitated the participation of women in the workplace for survival, the Africana woman has only recently been able to entertain the notion of spending more time at home with her family, either quantitatively or qualitatively. According to Blassingame:

> *On many plantations women did not have enough time to prepare breakfast in the morning and were generally too tired to make much of a meal or to give much attention to their children after a long day's labor. (180-81)*

Historically, the very presence of the Africana woman tracing back to the American slave experience in the new world was created from the exploited nature of the need of her workmanship away from "home" with no regard for her need and desire for familihood. She, like her male counterpart, was brought to America to work the fields. She did not have the privilege of remaining in the home like White women did; her labor outside the home was mandated. In fact, long after slavery, all too frequently she could find labor when her male counterpart could not. It has been conjectured that Africana males were disallowed stable employment within the capitalist system, and Africana women were allowed gainful employment as a tactic by the dominant culture to further emasculate Africana men, thereby causing confusion and disharmony within the Africana family structure. Africana men were often left with the insecurity of joblessness, which did nothing for their self-esteem. In a traditional male-dominated society, men have always been expected to be the bread-winners, not the women. Since the reverse became the reality in the Africana family, the end result was the ultimate breakdown of the Africana family and spirit.

In spite of this reality, the greatest concern of the Africana woman has always been her family. Therefore, unlike the feminist, who discourages emphasis on the family if it "becomes an instrument of oppression and denial of individual rights" (Klatch 128), the Africana woman is less inclined to focus primarily on herself and her career at the expense of the family and its needs. Granted, she is concerned with her career, as it is the very means by which she can contribute to the support of her family. The notion of self as a primary issue and family as a lesser priority is unfounded and unworkable in the reality of the Africana woman. The movement of the Africana womanist today, then, is from the workplace to the home-place, at least spiritually, in the sense of where her heart and spirit rest regarding the importance of her family and home.

In Concert with Males in Struggle

The Africana womanist is also in concert with males in the broader struggle for humanity and the liberation of all Africana people. The idea of the intertwined destiny of Africana men, women, and children is directly related to the notion of the dependency upon the male sector in the participation of the Africana womanist's struggle for herself and her family. Unlike the mainstream feminist, whose struggle is characteristically independent of and oftentimes adverse to male participation, the Africana womanist invites her male counterpart into her struggle for liberation and parity in society, as this struggle has been traditionally the glue that has held them together and enabled them to survive in a particularly hostile and racist society.

A close look at and consideration of the dynamics of feminism clearly reveal some rather shocking, disconcerting, and even threatening consequences if left unaddressed, particularly in regard to Africana women. Given the obvious and not-so-obvious tensions resulting from sexual inequity or gender competition, grounded in a traditionally White-male-dominated society, feminism does ostensibly offer a possible solution to the problem confronting females in general. However, the possible solution, as perceived by the feminist, to the long-existing and neglected threat to the freedom and dignity of the woman does not come without sacrifices to her community. For example, the numerous append-ages to the term feminist, such as radical feminist separatist, cultural feminist, post-structural feminist, and lesbian, suggest a quasi-exclusive membership, one that often exudes an intolerance of men in general. According to Nicholas Davidson in *The Failure of Feminism*:

> *The feminist perspective imposes a one-dimensional interpretation on all aspects of human life, namely, that evils of the world can all be traced to men oppressing women. It generates female chauvinism and sex-hate mongering.* (296)

For the White feminist, separation from the male sector, psychologically, emotionally, and/or physically, as a survival strategy is essential in order for her to become whole. This is not the case for the Africana womanist. Paula Giddings observes that:

> *A ... disquieting aspect of the women's movement was the shrill tone it adopted against men. Inherent in this, of course, was the prevailing attitude among White women that sexism was the enemy. Black women, far more concerned about the impress of racism on their lives, believed that racial oppression was the root of their problems.* (309)

The notion of challenging the applicability and viability of feminism as it relates to and operates within the constructs of the Africana woman's experience and her family does not mean that Africana women and white women do not share critical gender issues that need be resolved. Nor is it to suggest that confronting these concerns in general (particularly in terms of the manner in which the feminist handles them, which too frequently erupts into alienation from the opposite sex) is to be interpreted as anti-feminist. The critical concern here is how the problem is to be resolved, with specific reference to the exclusion of the very instrument of female subjugation, the male, who, in the final analysis, obviously needs himself to be corrected and redeemed. Africana women, instead of addressing relational conflicts between Africana men and themselves by excluding the former, work toward resolving the tension via working together with mutual respect, with a realization that Nigerian businesswoman Ajai comes to that Africana women's "emancipation is unattainable until the basic rights are provided all people" (Quoted in Ntiri's *One Is Not A Woman, One Becomes*, 6).

While the White man may very well be the enemy of the White woman in her struggle, the Africana man does not necessarily hold that position against the Africana woman. An Africana Womanist Movement, then, could possibly close the gender gap and heal the wounds of both genders so that they could more collectively work toward ameliorating the life-threatening social ills for Africana people in particular and people in general in our world today. Considering the worsening collective plight of Black people, they cannot afford to have their attention deflected and focus on gender-based animosities. This is not to say that there is no room for discussion of issues relating to interactions between Africana men and women, for Africana men have unfortunately internalized the White patriarchal system to some degree. Ultimately, the collective survival of Africanans should be the primary concern. If Samuel Yette's observations of the inevitability of Black genocide in *The Choice* were to come true, it is doubtful that a situation would develop whereby only Africana men or only Africana women would be taken to concentration camps and the other gender spared.[3] Just to universalize the issue, the dominant culture is not likely to distinguish between the sexes where annihilation of an entire race is the issue. Africana men and women share a similar space as oppressed people, and thus, they cannot afford this division between the sexes.

Flexible Role Players

Another characteristic of the Africana womanist is flexible role-playing. This is a controversial topic today due to the predicament of the Africana man and woman, which dates back to American slavery, when neither partner was free to act out the defined roles of men and women as set forth by the dominant culture. The Africana woman has never been restricted to the home and household chores, and her male counterpart has more often than not shared the role as homemaker.

According to Sara Evans, the roles in the Africana community have always been nearly indistinguishable. For example, Africana women have not had the long-standing role as "only" homemaker, a traditional role from which White women look forward to retiring:

> *Certain differences result from the way in which Black women grow up. We have been raised to function independently. The notion of retiring to housewifery someday is not even a reasonable fantasy. Therefore whether you want to or not, it*

is necessary to learn to do all of the things required to do to survive. It seemed to many of us, on the other hand, that white women were demanding a chance to be independent while we needed help and assistance that was not always forthcoming. We definitely started from opposite ends of the spectrum ... we did the same work as men ... usually with men. (239-40)

Africana men, too, have not had the consistent experience of upholding the traditional role of the male as the head of the household. In a traditional patriarchal system the male is expected to fulfill the responsibilities outside the home, such as earning money, while serving as the official head inside the home. On the home base, he dictates the order of the household and designates the woman to carry it out. This woman, under the direction of her husband, is expected to be of a particular type. Today the mainstream feminist dismantles, or in some instances inverts the traditional roles in general, and redefines the male and female roles in society as anything but traditional. Redefined sexual roles for feminists remain at the forefront of their movement. On the other hand, to some degree, the Africana womanist accepts the traditional roles, some of which are valid and appropriate, since obviously there are some distinctions between the sexes, such as the biological difference between men and women. Women cannot share their biological role as child-bearer, and men are still considered the protectors in most circles, and are expected to uphold the family and defend, physically if need be, both their women and children. Although Africana women do believe in and respect traditional roles, it must be established that those roles, for Africana women and men alike, have never been so clearly defined in the Africana community and thus, the roles have always been somewhat relaxed.

Genuine Sisterhood

There has always been bonding among Africana women that cannot be broken—genuine sisterhood. This sisterly bond is a reciprocal one, one in which each gives and receives equally. In this community of women, all reach out in support of each other, demonstrating a tremendous sense of responsibility for each other by looking out for one another.

They are joined emotionally, as they embody empathic understanding of each other's shared experiences. Everything is given out of love, criticism included, and in the end, the sharing of the common and individual experiences and ideas yields rewards.

There is no substitute for sisterhood, and while the traditional family is of key importance to the Africana womanist, she recognizes her need for this genuine connection between women, one that supports her in her search for solace in her time of need, and offers insight in her time of confusion. While there have been attempts to define all types of female relationships, lesbian relationships included, as a form of sisterhood, this particular kind of sisterhood refers specifically to an asexual relationship between women who confide in each other and willingly share their true feelings, their fears, their hopes, and their dreams. Enjoying, understanding, and supporting each other, women friends of this sort are invaluable to each other. With such love, trust and security, it is difficult to imagine any woman without such a genuine support system as that found in genuine sisterhood.

Strong

Generally speaking, the Africana womanist comes from a long tradition of psychological as well as physical strength. She has persevered centuries of struggling for herself and her family. The ultimate example of her strength is how she has both endured and survived slavery, suffering the unimaginably cruel enforced separation from her family. Welch contends

> *I find in many of their lives, and reflected in their writings, a moral wisdom that I wish to study and to emulate, a tradition of strength and persistence that is one of the richest heritages of humankind. (16)*

Witnessing and understanding her male counterpart's powerlessness and his inability to fulfill the traditional role of the man as protector, resulting in his emasculation, the Africana womanist has continued to demonstrate her strength and steadfastness in protecting the vulnerabilities of her family. Reflecting upon her historical strength, particularly during the time when Africana people experienced the most severe blows of servitude, she embraces with open arms the rich legacy of her sisters' enduring strength out of both awesome courage and true love for her family. Thus, the Africana womanist lives on.

Male Compatible

The Africana womanist desires positive male companion-ship, a relationship in which each individual is mutually supportive, an important part of a positive Africana family. According to African writer Elechi Amadi, "men and women need each other emotionally and, of course, for survival" (*Ethics in Nigerian Culture*, 71). In the Africana community, neither women nor men can afford to conclude that the other gender was irredeemable and therefore, undesirable. Such a stance of totally disregarding or dismissing the other gender could resort in racial suicide for Africana people. Note that in the midst of the experiences of strong Africana women being abandoned by men, there are millions of Africana women with entirely different experiences, those who praise their hard-working husbands and fathers who got no recognition. These stories or cases have somehow been overlooked in the historical perspective. To be sure, positive male companionship is of great interest to the Africana womanist in general, for she realizes that male and female relationships are not only comforting but the key to perpetuating the human race. Without each other, the human race becomes extinct.

The Africana womanist also realizes that, while she loves and respects herself and is, in general, at peace with herself, she ultimately desires a special somebody to fill a void in her life, one who makes her complete. Novelist Terry McMillan considers many Africana women's desire for male companionship and comments on the void in their lives:

> We don't have a husband or a steady man in our lives, though most of us would like to ... We spend too many precious hours on the phone, over dinner—everywhere —discussing the problems and perils of wanting, loving and needing black men. (McMillan, "Hers")

The Africana womanist is in search of a positive male/female relationship experience. However, merely settling for companionship for the sake of having a man is the farthest thing from the best-case scenario of the true Africana womanist.

Respected and Recognized

The Africana womanist, above all, demands respect for and recognition of herself in order to acquire true self-esteem and self-worth, which in turn enables her, among other things, to have complete and positive relationships with all people. According to Crooks and Baur in *Our Sexuality*, "when people feel secure in their own worth and identity, they are able to establish intimacy with others" (238). If the Africana woman lacks self-love, which can result from accepting the White standard of beauty[4] she will inevitably exude a negative sense of herself, thereby assuming a "zero image."[5] This negative self-image could possibly result in her allowing herself to be disrespected, abused, and trampled on by her male counterpart. Because this sometimes happens, no one can realistically deny that gender issues do not constitute critical concern in the Africana community. And by the same token, no thinking Africana person can disagree with Doreatha Drummond Mbalia in *Toni Morrison's Developing Class Consciousness* "that the gender oppression of African [Africana] women is the result of the African [Africana] male's class exploitation and race oppression" (17). We are, after all, still both Africanan and people, operating within the constructs of a basically White patriarchal system, and thus, we are not free from contamination of female oppression. But it cannot be overemphasized that the Africana woman must seek feasible ways of combating this triple problem from within her own community. Sexism is clearly not the most critical issue for the Africana womanist. Unquestionably, the salient phenomenon that plagues the Africana community is poverty, in which racism plays a major part, and out of this poverty come crime and death. Be that as it may, whether it is a problem of race, class, or sex, the Africana woman must insist upon both respect of her person and recognition of her humanness so that she may more effectively fulfill her role as a positive and responsible co-partner in the overall Africana struggle. The Africana man, too, must do his part, beginning with total respect for his female counterpart. If he disrespects his women, he disrespects self in a real sense.

Whole and Authentic

The true Africana womanist seeks both wholeness (completeness) and authenticity (cultural connection) in her life. Understandably by now she wants it all, or at least as much as she can assist in achieving. That means she wants her home, her family and her career, neglecting no one of these for the others. Granted, the family does come first in priority for the Africana woman, but the other things are very much needed and extremely important, as they come together to ensure harmony and security in the home.

In acquiring wholeness, the Africana womanist demonstrates her desire for a positive male companionship, for without her male counterpart, her life is not complete in a real sense. She needs male companionship and likewise, he needs female companionship. Both are essential to the survival of the human race. Her sense of wholeness is necessarily compatible with her cultural consciousness and authentic existence. As an authentic being, her standards, her acts, and her ideals directly reflect those dictated by her own culture. Hence, her true essence compliments her culture, thereby denying any room for an inauthentic self. Collectively, wholeness and authenticity are powerful tenets of the Africana womanist; her heritage also strongly stresses the importance of an entire family unit.

Spirituality

The Africana womanist demonstrates a definite sense of spirituality, a belief in a higher power that transcends rational ideals, which is an ever-present part of Africana culture. From this point of reference, she acknowledges the existence of spiritual reality, which brings into account the power of comprehension, healing, and the unknown. A natural phenomenon, spirituality cannot be omitted from the character of Africana women, "whose spirituality," according to Alice Walker, "was so intense, so deep, so unconscious, that they were themselves unaware of the richness they held" (232-33). In almost every aspect of the Africana womanist's life, she bears out and bears witness to, either consciously or subconsciously, this aspect of African cosmology. When one looks at her in making everyday decisions, one senses her reliance upon the inner spirit or mind. In the area of health care, she frequently goes back to folk medicine and spiritual healing, such as the laying on of hands, which entails her placing her hands on another while praying for his or her healing. Moreover, she is connected to the spiritual world and with undaunted faith she is often spiritually guided by those of that world. In African cosmology, the physical and spiritual world co-exist and hence, both realities compliment each other in working for the good of all in the universe.

Respectful of Elders

The true African womanist respects and appreciates elders, insisting that her young do likewise, for Africana elders have served as role models and have paved the way for future generations. This respect and appreciation for elders is another continuum of African culture, which Africana women still demonstrate and insist upon in their everyday lives. They protect their elders and seek their advice, as the wisdom of elders is indisputable. Elders, in general, have been an integral part of Africana family-hood, and have themselves continued to strengthen the family by physical and/or spiritual participatory activities. As a spiritual and religious people, Africana women have been taught to practice the greatest regard for elders, for they are the mothers and fathers of our community. If one cannot respect the parents, one cannot be expected to respect anyone, self included. Thus, Africana women out of both habit and consciousness have deep reverence, genuine love and compassion for their elders.

Adaptable

The true Africana womanist demands no separate space for nourishing her individual needs and goals, while in the twentieth-century feminist movement, there is the White feminist's insistence upon personal space. One of the leading mainstream feminists, Virginia Woolf, insists that women must have their separate space, preferably a place away from home, in order for them to be truly creative.[4] A woman must have, she feels, a room of her own, a place to escape to, for success and creativity. This could allow the intellectual freedom that depends upon material things, which comments upon the necessity of economic freedom. A separate space for most Africana women, as well as for lower-working-class women in general, is not only impossible but inconceivable. These women in general often have limited funds. Taking those funds to defray expenses for a separate space, which necessarily means renting a place and hiring a sitter for the children in most cases, would in effect mean taking the necessities from the family. Needless to say, this is not the common reality of Africana woman. However, the absence of a separate space does not render her non-creative, neither does it render her unsuccessful.

Ambitious

Ambition and responsibility are highly important in the life of the Africana womanist, for her family, too, depends on these qualities in her. From early on, the Africana woman is taught the importance of self-reliance and resourcefulness, and hence, she makes a way out of no way, creating ways to realize her goals and objectives in life. The sense of responsibility she has for her family is paramount and so she creates a private space for herself in the midst of chaos, confusion, and congestion, even while washing dishes, feeding the baby, or cooking dinner. It may be in a tiny room, or a closet, or it may be in the wee hours after bedtime for her family, but not a totally separate space away from her family. Whatever the case, the Africana woman, with ingenuity, provides herself with whatever is necessary for her creative energies to soar. Thus, within the walls of some Africana homes lurk many perceptive and creative Africana women writers, for example, workers, without rooms of their own, who explore their myriad experiences in attempts to create some artistic semblance of their realities, perspectives, and possibilities regarding the status of the Africana community—its women, its men, and its children. In the final analysis, the Africana womanist is her own person, fully equipped with her own problems, her own successes, her own set of priorities.

Mothering and Nurturing

Finally, the Africana womanist is committed to the art of mothering and nurturing, her own children in particular and humankind in general. This collective role is supreme in Africana culture, for the Africana woman comes from a legacy of fulfilling the role of supreme Mother Nature—nurturer, provider, and protector. There is a historical emphasis on the importance of motherhood in Africa, since the structure of the family in many countries was polygamous. Historically, the role of mother was more important than the role of wife, for example. The Africana woman operates from within these constructs. Unlike many White feminists quoted in Davidson's *The Failure of Feminism*, such as Kate Millet (who calls for the abolition of the traditional role of the mother), Germaine Greer (who expounds upon the crucial plight of mothers), Betty Rollin (who contends that motherhood is none other than a concept adopted from society by women), and Betty Friedan (who pleads the case of pathology in children of careerless, overprotective mothers), the Africana womanist comes from a legacy of dedicated wives and mothers. And thus, according to Algea Harrison:

> *Black women have consistently indicated that they value the role of mother and consider it an important aspect of their sex role identity. Indeed there was evidence that Black women sometimes prioritized the mother role over wife and worker roles. (204)*

The Africana womanist is committed to loving and caring for her own, which extends to the entire Africana family. Enjoying her role, she both encourages her own and sacrifices herself in executing her duty to humankind. She is consistent in doing what must be done for the survival of the family, a commitment grounded in and realized through a positive sense of history, familihood, and security, all of which true mothering and nurturing provide, and which the true Africana womanist embodies.

In conclusion, the key descriptors of the Africana womanist are very important, as they bring forth a holistic existence for both her and her family. Refining a paradigm relative to who the Africana womanist is and has always been could enable us to better resolve the existing conflict between the Africana and particularly the gap characterizing modern-day male/female relationships. Once this is resolved, we could witness a beautiful union between the genders that would inevitable bring about a harmonious world for all.

END NOTES

1 This quote comes from 'Zulu Sofola in her paper entitled "Feminism and the Psyche of African Womanhood," which was delivered at the International Conference on Women of Africa and the African Diaspora, July 1992.

2 At the 1992 International Conference on Women of Africa and the African Diaspora, Rose Acholonu made this statement in her paper entitled, "Love and the Feminist Utopia."

3 See Samuel Yette's *The Choice* for further discussion on Black genocide.

4 Read Toni Morrison's *The Bluest Eye* for further insights into the devastating impact of buying into an alien standard of beauty. For a detailed analysis of this novel and this phenomenon, see Chapter Two—"The Damaging Look: The Search for Authentic Existence in *The Bluest Eye*"—in Wilfred Samuels and Clenora Hudson-Weems' *Toni Morrison*.

5 The "zero image" is a term coined by Carolyn Gerald in "The Black Writer and His Role" in Addison Gayle's *The Black Aesthetics*.

6 For further discussion on Virginia Woolf's theory of "separate space," see her book entitled *A Room of One's Own*.

BIBLIOGRAPHY

Ajai, Taiwo. "The Voluptuous Ideal" in *One Is Not a Woman, One Becomes: The African Woman in a Transitional Society.* Daphne Williams Ntiri, ed. Troy: MI: Bedford, 1982, 77-87.

Amadi, Elechi. *Ethic in Nigerian Culture.* Ibadan: Heinemann, 1982.

Asante, Molefi Kete. Afterword in *Africana Womanist Literary Theory* by Clenora Hudson-Weems, 2004. Trenton, New Jersey: Africa World Press, 2004, 137-139.

Blassingame, John W. *The Slave Community: Plantation Life in the Antebellum South.* New York: Oxford University Press, 1979.

Christian, Barbara. *Black Feminist Criticism: Perspectives on Black Women Writers.* New York: Pergamon, 1985.

Crooks, Robert and Karla Baur. *Our Sexuality.* Redwood City, CA: Benjamin/Cumming, 1990.

Davidson, Nicholas. *The Failure of Feminism.* Amherst, New York: Prometheus Books, 1988.

Evans, Sara. *Personal Politics: The Roots of Women's Liberation in the Civil Rights Movement and the new Left.* New York: Knopf, 1979.

Franklin, John Hope and Alfred A. Moss, Jr. *From Slavery to Freedom: A History of Negro Americans*, 6th ed. New York: McGraw-Hill, 1988.

Gerald, Carolyn F. "The Black Writer and His Role." *The Black Aesthetics.* Addison Gayle, ed. New York: Doubleday (1997), 349-56.

Giddings, Paule. *When and Where I Enter: The Impact of Black Women on Race and Sex in America.* New York: Bantam, 1984.

Hall, Leland K. "Support Systems and Coping Patterns." *Black Men.* Lawrence E. Gary, ed. Beverly Hills: *Sage,* 1981.

Harrison, Algea. "Attitudes Toward Procreation among Black Adults." *Black Families,* Harriette Pipes McAdoo, ed. Beverly Hills, London: *Sage,* 1981, 199-208.

Klatch, Rebecca E. *Women of the New Right.* Philadelphia: Temple University Press, 1987.

Mbalia, Doreatha Drummond. *Toni Morrison's Developing Class Consciousness.* Selinsgrove, PA: Susquehanna University Press, 1991.

McMillan, Terry. "Hers," in *The New York Times.* October 15, 1987.

Morrison, Toni. *The Bluest Eye.* New York: Holt, Rinehart, & Winston, 1970.

Steady, F.C. ed. *The Black Woman Cross-Culturally.* Rochester, VT: Schenkman Books, 1981.

Walker, Alice. *In Search of Our Mothers' Gardens.* San Diego: Harcourt, 1983.

Welch, Sharon D. *A Feminist Ethic of Risk.* Minneapolis: Fortress, 1990.

Wheeler, Barbara. "Africana Womanism, An African Legacy: It Ain't Easy Being a Queen." *Contemporary Africana Theory Thought and Action: A Guide to Africa Studies,* Clenora Hudson-Weems, ed. Trenton, New Jersey: Africa World Press, 2004, 319-331.

Woolf, Virginia. *A Room of One's Own.* New York: Harcourt, 1957.

Yette, Samuel F. *The Choice: The Issue of Black Survival in America.* Maryland: Cottage, 1971.

CHAPTER FOUR

The Africana Womanist Male Counterpart

It is fairly difficult to finalize the dynamics of the true Africana woman without giving some attention to her mal encounter part, the positive Africana man. It seems only plausible and natural that the Africana man would have characteristics commensurate with those of his counterpart. Thus, in observing positive Africana men, it becomes clear that positive Africana men share similar qualities with the Africana woman.

(AFRICANA WOMANISM 144)

The Africana male counterpart for the Africana woman calls for a focus at this juncture on looking at his make-up, particularly since our destinies are interconnected. Just as I have enumerated and expounded upon the eighteen (18) characteristics of the true Africana woman, I must likewise enumerate and define the eighteen (18) characteristics of the true Africana man, which are as follows:

Self-Namer

Like the Africana woman, the Africana man must be resolute in naming himself. You must never allow others to name you, as you, then, give them power over your life, your domain, and your destiny. Whenever someone takes the liberty of assigning your identity to you, without your permission, you must reject it and insist on claiming that privilege yourself. For example, too often are men called "dogs" by women who feel that is some way or another, they have been mistreated or disrespected by them. The connotation of such a term is loaded with negative meanings, such as low down and dirty, promiscuous, violent and uncaring. In actuality, for the most part, dogs are quite the opposite of what is inferred. For centuries they have been called "Man's best friend," as they have proven to be loyal, protective, faithful, and very affectionate. When others would abandon you, they would be there, right by your side. Thus, one must be careful not to trust others in the serious act of naming. It is a responsibility that you must insist upon keeping control of, or you may very well become what the name represents. Remember, in African cosmology, proper naming, *nommo*, is essential to existence.

Self-Definer

As critical to self-naming is self-defining, as they are inextricably linked together. Names and definitions are very difficult to separate, though terminology and meaning could have a slight difference. For example, a respected French linguist, Ferdinand de Saussure comments on the dynamics of language, which he contends does not convey reality. He asserts that language is a system of signs (words) and that inherent are both signifiers (signs/words) and the signified (the actual thing itself, regardless of the term assigned to it). Thus, utilizing or assigning a word to a thing does not create that which the word suggests. As the old saying goes "A rose by any other name is still a rose." That said, we must be careful on the matter of definitions to ensure accuracy.

Family-Centered

The true Africana man must be family-centered, as his family should be his number one priority. The man, generally referred to as the head of the household, must assume the responsibility of the safety and security of his family. His family depends upon him for guidance and strength, but it is important to know and understand that his female counterpart has the responsibility to share those family concerns with him. As his co-partner, she must be by his side to uphold those things necessary for the survival of their family, realizing that together they can make almost anything happen. Senegalese writer Mariama Bâ makes an excellent case of family centrality in her epistolary novel, *So Long a Letter*. *Africana Womanism: Reclaiming Ourselves*, Chapter Six does a great job interpreting this characteristic in the primary concern of the protagonist, Ramatoulaye, who "delivers one of the most powerful and positive commentaries on male/female relationships within the context of human existence and the role of familihood" (Hudson-Weems, *Africana Womanism*, 102).

Role Model

Important to any group are good role models. They stand as examples of how we must be, how we think and how we act. For the Africana man, he must represent the positive of which the woman is proud and to which the children can aspire. In short, he should be someone that all should be proud to be a part of their lives. In Toni Morrison's *Beloved*, though late for the protagonist, Sethe, Paul D. represents the supreme paradigm of a positive male role model. He cares for not only his woman, but for her family as well and wants only the best for her, always insisting that "You your best thing, Sethe. You are" (Morrison 273).

Strong

Traditionally, the man represents the physical strength of the family. But like the Africana woman, he must exude both physical and emotional strength. While it is expected of him to use his physical prowess, to move object for example, it is not to be misused, such as to inflict violence on his female counterpart. When a man does this, he has, in actuality, violated the physical power God has given him for other purposes. If guilty of such perverse and cowardly acts, he can be assured that in time, he will experience retribution and/or abandonment in one form or another. As the male protagonists in Zora Neale Hurston's *Their Eyes Were Watching God* demonstrated in their chauvinistic behavior, subjugating the female protagonist, Janie Mae Crawford, in all three of her marriages, physical overpowering of the woman ultimately does nothing for their image. The Africana man must be strong and sure of himself, and not succumb to abusing his mate to make himself look stronger and, moreover, feel more in control. For more on this issue, consult the analysis of this novel in *Africana Womanism: Reclaiming Ourselves*, Chapter Five, entitled "Hurston's *Their Eyes Were Watching God: Seeking Wholeness.*

Committed to Struggle

The concerted efforts of the Africana man and woman are penultimate in our liberation struggle. Nothing could be more rewarding than the coming together of these two entities in working towards the success, happiness and overall well-being of the family and the community. This feature of the Africana man is further expounded upon in Chapter Six, "Africana Male-Female Relationships and Sexism in the Africana Community." A novel the prizes itself on the importance of this feature for both the Africana man and woman is Sister Souljah's *No Disrespect*, and Chapter Seven of *Africana Womanist Literary Theory*, "Sister Souljah's *No Disrespect*: The Africana Womanist's Dilemma," highlights this feature well as explicated in the following passage:

> *... The author establishes the fact that racism is the most critical issue confronting the Africana family, its past, its present and its future, which negatively affects our "ability to relate to and love one another in healthy life-giving relationships" (Souljah, xiv). ... Thus, she asserts she came to truly "understand how the day-to-day pressures of being black, penniless, structureless, culturally restricted, and frustrated in America could tear away at something that was supposed to be sacred: our loved ones and our family" (41). ... If we are true to our rich legacy of collectivity and familihood, we would accept ultimate responsibility for our lives, in spite of the negative role that others have played and continue to play in our lives. (Hudson-Weems, Africana Womanist, 100-101)*

Whole

Being a complete person, whole and well-rounded, is essential to love and happiness. The Africana man needs this quality in order that he may better relate and understand others. A one-dimensional personality is fragmented and cannot be trusted in a wholesome relationship that requires the totality of both parties. We need to see the depths of an individual, his physical and external being, as well as his emotional and internal make-up. We need to share all of this with our co-partners so that each can better cope with the adversities with which he/she is confronted both inside and outside the home-place.

Authentic

Authenticity is extremely important in assessing the true Africana family. It means that you are racially conscious and therefore, true to your culture, as being culturally connected makes you not only love yourself and your heritage, but protect and defend it as well. You will find yourself doing whatever it takes to improve the image of your race, which in not to be confused with inauthentic acts of assimilation. This is what too many Black people do, thinking that duplicating other's cultural values, such as those of the dominate culture, would make them better and more accepted and respected. Granted, unfortunately, there are some rewards that come with assimilation, but those rewards come as the sacrifice of one's self, indeed, a high price for surface gratification. For example, in Paule Marshall's *Praisesong for the Widow*, the protagonist,

> *Avey comes to realize that her formally socially accepted lifestyle as assimilationist . . . [and moreover] her earlier life with Jerome [her male counterpart] had been more authentic before they moved from Halsey Street to the all-White neighborhood in North White Plains (Hudson-Weems, Africana Womanism, 110).*

Flexible Role Player

In the Africana family, we must be flexible role players, for we are duties and obligations are not cast in stone. We have to shift or switch roles according to the needs and demands of the family. The Africana man and woman are co-partners and as such, they find themselves often having to cover each other's back, even to the extent of performing the traditionally assigned activities of the other. For example, if, for what ever reason, the man is at some time jobless, the woman must assume the role of primary bread-winner without feeling that he is less a man because of it. In Terry McMillan's *Disappearing Acts*, one of the two protagonist, the Africana man, "Franklin necessarily has to take care of the home, which he does well. . . . Franklin tries to accept their situation for the time being, but, of course, he has a difficult time not maintaining the traditional role of breadwinner" (139). The chapter, "McMillan's *Disappearing Acts*: In It Together" continues the Africana Womanist analysis with equal attention given to the Africana man.

Respectful of Women

What does it take for the Africana man to realize that to disrespect his woman is to disrespect himself and his whole race? She is the mother of his children, the mother of the race and as such, deserves respect. Granted, the respect for her should be reciprocal, but it should naturally start here.

A very strong Africana womanist, Dr. Regina Jennings, does an excellent inside assessment, as a member of the Party, of the Africana man and women in the Black Panther Party during its early years. In her article in a Special Issue on Africana Womanism for *The Western Journal of Black Studies* entitled "Africana Womanism in the Black Panther Party: A Personal Story," she exposes the sexist behavior of one man in particular, the captain whose acts represents disrespect for this female counterpart, which needed challenge:

> *There were women in the Party like me who tried to hold on because we understood the power, the significance and the need for our organization. Black men, who had been too long without some form of power, lacked the background to understand and rework their double standards toward the female cadre. Perhaps, if the Party had external observers—community elders who respected our platform—such unfair practices against women would not have occurred or could have been curbed.*

However, all men in the Party were not sexist, and I must emphasize this, for as an Africana womanist, I am interested in both the truth and in my total race. (Jennings, *WJBS*, 151).

Not only must Africana men respect his women, they must demand that others do so as well. Later in this book, Chapter Seven, entitled "In Response to Don Imus, 2007," I explored the dynamics of disrespect of the Africana woman, which has to cease. Without the respect for the Africana woman, the Africana man and our race are not going very far.

Protector

The Africana man must at all times protect his woman. He must stand by her side, ready to defend her in case of danger. This is not to suggest in any way that he must tower over her, dictating what she can or cannot do in terms of her choices or decision. It is only to assure her that her life is being guarded against any harm, hurt or danger. In short, the Africana man must have his female counterpart's back.

Responsibility goes hand and hand with the role of the Africana man as protector. He must be accountable for both the financial and emotional security of his children as a means of protecting them, too, from hurt and danger. The day of the single household, female mother-father, absentee father must be no more in the real sense. In other words, whether or not he is physically there at all times (the parents may have divorced or may have never married in the first place) should have very little or nothing to do with his responsibility to his children, as his presence in the sense of protecting and supporting them and their mother is penultimate for their future. Therefore, his involvement with his children in every sense is a requirement for the ultimate survival of our future generations. In order to move forward in a positive and progressive way, our children need first the survival of their family, at least in the sense of support, to which we must all aspire, including the fathers.

Moral

Morality is another important feature for the Africana man. He must know that doing the right thing, doing what is good is a great attribute. In the case of deciding upon and holding to the commitment to family, this is penultimate, as too often today, people fall into the snake pit of wallowing in the mud with people who are immoral who have no interest in or respect for the truly good things in life.

Female-Compatible

The cornerstone for the survival of the Africana family is male-female compatibility. Thus, for the Africana man, he must be female-compatible. He must love and honor his mate as the deserving precious jewel in his life. She would be the love of his life, as he should certainly be the love of her life. There is nothing more sacred and beautiful than a loving committed couple for the ultimate survival of the Africana family/community. Morrison's Sixo in *Beloved* comments on the beauty of such a relationship between the man and the woman:

> *"She is a friend of my mind. She gather me, man. The pieces I am, she gather them and give them back to me in all the right order. It's good, you know, when you got a woman who is a friend of your mind."* (Morrison 272-273)

Respectful of Elders

Much like this quality for the Africana womanist, the Africana man must demonstrate reverence and respect for his elders. They have been there for all of us from the beginning, and having paid their dues for humankind and particularly for our community, they are more than deserving of respect in their declining years on this earth.

Supportive

Support of your co-partner is a large part of what it takes to make for a positive relationship. That support is not only physical, but emotional and spiritual as well. Supporting each other on all levels, including also financially, socially and politically, in all of the family affairs and decisions, is mandatory. This is not to suggest that you support your partner in unwise matters and choices, for it will surely be the demise, rather than the fruition a successful union with longevity.

Ambitious

Everyone needs someone to share the financial responsibilities of the household, be that in the capacity of both having jobs and careers or in the capacity of one staying home to manage the finances. Whatever, the case, ambition is essential to helping to make ends meet for the security of the family. The Africana man must not fall prey to the jealousy monster and let go his own ambition due to the success of his mate. He must remain ever true to his own ambition to ensure that he has become all that he wants to be in life. This feature is well developed in Teri McMillan's *Disappearing Act*, which is analyzed from an Africana womanist perspective in *Africana Womanism: Reclaiming Ourselves*.

Fathering and Loving

Finally, in successful parenting, the last two features of the true Africana man, fathering and loving, go hand in hand. You must not be afraid of taking control in circumstances when the opinion and rules of the father are critical to decision making for the family. You must be firm in upholding the leadership role in the family, while at the same time show love and concern for your family, and particularly in this case, the children. In other words, the Africana man must demonstrate tough love when needed, in order for the child/children to grow up in a wholesome environment for a wholesome personal development. To be sure, loving and fathering are not to be feared, but rather revered.
(Hudson-Weems, *Africana Womanism*, 144)

In conclusion,

> *If all Africana men respected the original reality of the equality of both sexes in African cosmology, then they would refuse to continue to allow external forces, such as non-traditional African religions and alien political family structures wherein female subjugation is inherent, to influence their lives and ways. The end result would be that Africana people (men and women) the world over would then collectively struggle toward recovering their natural birth right as determiner of their fate as liberated people, dedicated to their families and their future generations* (Hudson-Weems, *Africana Womanism*, 144)

BIBLIOGRAPHY

Bâ, Mariama. *So Long a Letter*. Great Britain: Heinemman, 1989.

Hudson-Weems, Clenora. *Africana Womanism; Reclaiming Ourselves.* Troy, MI: Bedford, 1993.
_____. *Africana Womanist Literary Theory*. Trenton, New Jersey: Africa World Press, 2004.

Hurston, Zora Neale. *Their Eyes Were Watching God.* Urbana, IL: University of Illinois Press, 1978.

Jennings, Regina. "Africana Womanism in the Black Panther Party: A Personal Story" in *The Western Journal of Black Studies*, Volume 25, Number 3, Fall 2001, 146-152.

Marshall, Paule. *Praisesong for the Widow*. New York: A Dutton Belisk, 1984.

McMillan, Terry. *Disappearing Acts.* New York: Viking, 1989.

Morrison, Toni. *Beloved.* New York: Alfred A. Knopf, 1987.

Souljah, Sister. *No Disrespect.* New York: Vintage Books, 1996.

PART II

The Africana Family and a Call for Racial, Gender and Economic Parity

... Africana Womanism ... establishes an authentic race-based Africana theory of prioritizing race, class and gender for all women of African descent ... Black men and women must move forward together or the race will self-destruct.

(ALDRIDGE QUOTED IN THE DEFINITIVE EMMETT TILL, 151-2)

CHAPTER FIVE
Genuine Sisterhood or Lack Thereof

"Sula?" she whispered, gazing at the tops of trees. "Sula?'
Leaves stirred, mud shifted; there was the smell of overripe green
things. A soft ball of fur broke and scattered like dandelion spores in
the breeze.
"All that time, all that time, I thought I was missing Jude." And the
loss pressed down on her chest and came up into her throat. "We was
girls together," she said as though explaining something. "O Lord,
Sula," she cried, "girl, girl, girlgirlgirl."
It was a fine cry—loud and long—but it had no bottom and it had no
top, just circles and circles of sorrow. [Morrison, Sula, 149]

In this poignant closing pronouncement by speaker, Nel Wright, at the
grave site of her alter ego, Sula Peace, some twenty-five years after her
death, Toni Morrison makes a profound comment on the complexity and
value of a forever lost friendship between the two women in *Sula* (149).
As the author has proclaimed, she wanted to write about a profound
friendship between two women, and in spite of the complexity of that
relationship, which ostensibly appears to be problematic, particularly
since Sula has a sexual encounter with her best friend's husband, Jude, the
sum total of their experiences since their childhood could be expressed
as a metaphor for true genuine sisterhood.

Genuine sisterhood, which could be a catalyst by which other
Africana womanist qualities might be advanced to a higher lever, is one
of the eighteen characteristics of Africana Womanism as defined by

Hudson-Weems in *Africana Womanism*. It is one of the key components for human survival, for the security and harmony of women undergird the strength and structure of society and all its participants. In other words, women are the very foundation of life, whether they know it or not, and thus, they have to be a positive force in life for the ultimate survival of us all. Thus, as the late 'Zula Sofola asserts "The female gender is the center of life, the magnet that holds the social cosmos intact and alive. Destroy her and you destroy life itself" (*Africana Womanism* xviii). By extension, when we destroy each other, we also destroy humanity since we are, in fact, the backbone of humanity.

Much debate has taken place on the issue of sisterhood, which has been defined as

> *a reciprocal [bond] . . . in which each gives and receives equally. In this community of women, all reach out in support of each other, demonstrating a tremendous sense of responsibility for each other by looking out for one another. They are joined emotionally, as they embody empathic understanding of each other's shared experiences. Everything is given out of love, criticism included, and in the end, the sharing of the common and individual experiences and ideas yield rewards. . . . This particular kind of sisterhood refers specifically to an asexual relationship between women who confide in each other and [who] willingly share their true feelings--their fears, their hopes, and their dreams. [Hudson-Weems 65].*

The critical need for genuine sisterhood, which is essential for a positive society, cannot be over emphasized, for it is important for women, the family nucleus, to be able to communicate and assist each other in everyday decisions and activities. It is always advantageous to have someone to talk to, someone who is concerned about your needs, someone to give and receive positive feedback and action, both on a personal and a professional basis. As one writer notes, "Black women have a long and colorful tradition of gathering together. Black women are coming together in search of the kind of nurturing, caring and supportive talk that often only another black woman can provide" (Villarosa 82). Given the triple role that the Africana womanist must play--mother, partner and breadwinner--it is very difficult to separate her personal and professional worlds; thus, she needs that support system. To be sure, when one area is neglected, the other suffers as well; when one area soars, the other soars as well. In short, coming from a family-centered reality, the Africana womanist cannot effectively divorce herself from her family, as her job/career is not only important to her but to her family as well. That is to say, both her worlds usually rise or fall together. Significantly, it is often her female support system, or lack thereof, rendering or denying psychological and physical assistance that either helps or hinders in bringing her immediate or life goals to fruition. The Africana womanist, then, "recognizes her need for this genuine connection between women, one that supports her in her search for solace in her time of need, and offers insights in her time of confusion" (Hudson-Weems, 65). Their bonding renders one sure way of binging about ultimate success, for the sharing of one's life experiences often gives what is needed for that success. Hence, where there is a coming together of body, mind, and spirit, there is victory, and Africana women in today's society have much to overcome, given that they are, indeed, victims of a three-fold form of oppression—racism, classism, and sexism.

Another excellent literary example of sisterhood is demonstrated in the short epistolary novel *So Long A Letter*, by the Senegalese writer Mariama Bâ. The novel's protagonist, Ramatoulaye, embodies many characteristics of the true Africana womanist, the most obvious ones being genuine in sisterhood, and in family-centeredness. Beginning with the epistolary form of the work itself, its shape takes the form of letter writing between two women. And thereby displays a strong and reliable friendship, that demonstrates a genuineness in sisterhood. Within the friendship the protagonist finds a strong support system that enables her to withstand adversity. The very structure of the novel commands a bond of trust between writer and receiver, which we witness in operation between the protagonist Ramatoulaye and her confidante Aissatou (Hudson-Weems 96-97).

This eighty-five-page letter represents the ultimate in genuine sisterly solidarity:

> *The kind of friendship these women have goes beyond confiding in one another and sharing commonalities. Not only do they*

share their feelings, they share material things as well. . . . But
there is more. Beyond the sharing is the total empathy that
genuine sisterhood brings. While many are able to sympathize
with the suffering of others, very few are able to truly empathize
with another's pain [Hudson-Weems 97-98]

The quotation below from the novel itself, demonstrates the level of profound, lasting friendship the two women share as Ramotoulaye recounts the support she receives from her best friend after her husband, Modou, deserts her and their children for Bientou, a classmate and friend of one of their teenage daughter's:

"I shall never forget you response, you, my sister, nor my joy and
my surprise when I was called to the Fiat agency and was told
to choose a car which you had paid for, in full. My children gave
cries of joy when they learned of the approaching end of their
tribulations, which remain the daily lot of a good many other
students.
Friendship has splendors that love knows not. It grows stronger
when crossed, whereas obstacles kill love. Friendship resists
time, which wearies and severs couples. It has heights unknown
to love.
You, the goldsmith's daughter, gave me your help while depriving
yourself.
Your disappointment was mine, as my rejection was yours.
Forgive me once again if I have re-opened your wound. Mine
continues to bleed." [Bâ 53-55]

Indeed, this is the supreme paradigm of genuine sisterhood, which we need and would like to see again and again, particularly given the magnitude of stress that Africana women experience daily in a hostile, racist, white male-dominated society. We need to come together and share experiences in order to endure and to withstand the everyday sufferings that life holds. Such a friendship as shared by Ramatoulaye and Aissatou "enables the women to put life into proper perspective and establish order in their lives" (Hudson-Weems 98). It enables sisters to regroup and to refuel so that they can reemerge as positive strong

Africana women, continuing the legacy of togetherness and respect for one another.

Another model example of strong sisterly bonding is the ideal sisterhood between the title character of Gloria Naylor's *Mama Day* and her blood sister, Abigail, of Willow Springs. These loving sisters consult each other on all matters of importance. They talked to each other before making decisions even in seemingly unimportant matters. In fact, Miranda alias "Mama Day" greets her sister each morning, affectionately referring to her as "sister," and in every way that sacred title was respected. Yet another literary example of strong sisterhood is presented in Zora Neale Hurston's signature novel *Their Eyes Were Watching God*, in where the protagonist, Janie Mae Crawford, and her best friend and confident, Phoeby Watson, engage is an extraordinary sisterly relationship. In fact, it is Phoeby to whom Janie relates her complete heart wrenching continuous love story of her woes and joys with two male chauvinist husbands, "before she finally discovers 'Mr. Right" [Vergible "Tea Cake" Woods], the one man who can respect her as his equal" (Hudson-Weems 79). She trusts her empirically, giving Phoebe the option to tell or to protect her story, which ever she feels is best: "You can tell'em what Ah say if you wants to. Dat's just de same as me 'cause mah tongue is in mah friend's mouf." (Hurston 6). Countering this sisterly bond as the polar opposite is the situation in which the women in the community do not demonstrate love for one another, particularly toward Janie. Expressing her inability to treat Janie kindly because Janie's beauty reminds her of what she lacks.

Although it is evident that women do, in fact, need female bonding in order to give them the strength to continue, most often they do not truly relate to each other in the desired sisterly manner. In our modern-day society, women claim sisterhood as if it is a commonplace phenomenon, knowing full well that the term "sister" is too frequently used lightly or superficially, often without real commitment or sincerity. In other words, contrary to the use of the term in the early sixties and seventies, when women did in fact relate to each other in a more sisterly manner, the term itself has become more of a fashionable rather than a genuine utterance. One need only listen to the national popular dialogue on black women as phenomenon "sisters" and note the publications on the subject to concur that the idea of sisterhood has been too generalized, popularized, and sensationalized as one of the most in vogue colloquialisms today. To be sure, no matter the age, the race, or the class level, today's women treat each other in ways that insult the true idea of sisterhood, as the desired "bonds are often broken or slackened by competitiveness, betrayal, and physical or socioeconomic separation" (Andrews 1). Thus, they gossip about, conspire against, and even callously exclude each other by alienation, one of the most dreaded forms of emotional abuse. Consequently, many women shrink into themselves with an unimaginable sense of paranoia and insecurity, ultimately resulting in not only a distrust of women in particular, but more importantly, a distrust of humankind in general.

Although we would all like to see more sisterhood among women, this ideal unfortunately is not the norm. In order to achieve this goal, however, we must first candidly analyze the facts. The main culprit in female betrayal is disrespect, under which fall most of the Seven Deadly Sins (pride, avarice, wrath, envy, sloth, gluttony, and lechery). We disrespect and disregard each other's personhood with the individualistic notion that the most important thing in life is self. Moreover, our inflated egos frequently hinder us in extending ourselves to others, particularly in time of need. Thus, as Morrison confesses in her powerful commencement address, delivered at Barnard College in the 1980s,

> I am alarmed by the violence that women do to each other: professional violence, competitive violence, emotional violence. I am alarmed by the willingness of women to enslave other women. I am alarmed by a growing absence of decency on the killing floor of professional women's worlds. ("Cinderella's Stepsisters" 283).

What better way to express the urgent and crucial need for sisterhood in our competitive world of envy and incivility toward each other than in Morrison's indictment offered here. Commenting on her amazement at the cruel manner that women treat each other every day, particularly in the workplace, she offers profound insights into the true nature and source of the absence of sisterhood on the part of many women towards each other, an unfortunate phenomenon that violates the very foundation of female relationships. Moreover, in our pride and self-centeredness, we disallow ourselves a sense of humility that would enable us to apologize, particularly when we have miserably wronged each another. Refusal to apologize when warranted could conceivably result in the loss of a potentially life-long friendship simply because of over weaning pride.

Another human frailty, greed, results in placing too much emphasis on material gains. For example, we go to any lengths to accumulate wealth, including selfishly hoarding resources. In so doing, we refuse to share and network among ourselves, fearing that others could possibly benefit while lessening our own individual gains. Moreover, we often avoid helping each other because too many of those on top condescend and shun those on the bottom rather than reach back to bring those less fortunate sisters forward for the ultimate improvement of all. In confronting this problem, Morrison offers the following:

> *I am suggesting that we pay as much attention to our nurturing sensibilities as to our ambition. We are moving in the direction of freedom, and the function of freedom is to free somebody else. You are moving toward self-fulfillment, and the consequences of that fulfillment should be to discover that there is something just as important as you are and that just-as-important thing may be Cinderella—or your stepsister. [283]*

Never has this sin been more prevalent than it is today in the competitive world of the workplace, where base betrayal and socioeconomic separation take place. And never has it been more urgent than now to correct this flaw in ourselves if we expect to move forward in this new millennium positively.

Sometimes out of sheer animosity, we gossip and denigrate each other. Out of personal resentment and frustration with ourselves, and the world, we bitterly say cruel things about our sisters. Oftentimes this is because of petty jealousy that we complain of not liking a particular sister simply because of the way that she looks, talks, or presents herself. Remember, it is Shakespeare's Othello, whom Iago ironically warns-- "Beware ... the green-ey'd monster which doth mock/the meat it feeds on" (*Othello* 3.3.165-67). Out of professional envy, we begrudge each other's successes or cannot bring ourselves to acknowledge the other's accomplishments with simple congratulations believing that somehow giving a fellow sister recognition would somehow diminish our own importance. It may very well be that the heart of the matter is low self-esteem or lack of self-confidence, deficiencies--the tendency to diminish another who may vulnerably stand as yet another victim of individual malice--that could be corrected and hopefully ended forever.

Morrison, reflecting on the many disservices by women against women daily, both inside and outside the workplace, offers possible solutions to this problem, while demanding that evil towards fellow sisters cease:

> *I want not to ask you but to tell you not to participate in the oppression of your sisters. Mothers who abuse their children are women, and another woman, not an agency, has to be willing to stay their hands. Mothers who set fire to school buses are women, and another woman, not an agency, has to tell them to stay their hands. Women who stop the promotion of other women in careers are women, and another woman must come to the victim's aid. Social and welfare workers who humiliate their clients may be women, and other women colleagues have to deflect their anger. [283]*

Here she urges women to embrace each other with love and concern, rather than oppress each other out of confusion, jealousy, or anger. She comments on the fact that all too often we, as a part of the community of women, relate negatively to each other, which consequentially results in our missing out on the many good things that life has to offer. It is true that if we but reach out to each other, the world would be a much better place to live. Everyone would come out the winner, for in doing good, good, in turn, would inevitably come back to everyone. In this sense, we would experience <u>karma</u>, as postulated in Hindu philosophy, which is the relation between cause and effect, or in the case of individual ethical behavior, the governing factors for those relations. Hence, karma represents your getting back whatever is put forth, be it good or bad. In this same way, the Bible speaks of reaping what you sow. This idea could be extended to the specificity of women and their interaction with each other; therefore women should create for themselves, and for their fellow sisters and humankind alike, all the joys that life might possibly hold and in return offer them. We, as sisters, must shield ourselves and each other from many of life's misfortunes, many of which stem from various forms of abuse, betrayal, and alienation. If one were to really consider the phenomenon of female self-inflicted victimization, one might agree that we are, indeed, responsible for both ourselves, and each other, for both our fortunes and our misfortunes. In assuming that responsibility, we might ultimately end victoriously, as it might result in making possible the most significant victory that we, as individuals or as a collective, could hope to realize--the fruition of ultimate joy.

When something goes wrong, the first step toward correcting it is admitting that the problem exists. Hence, perception must meet reality. Too frequently we are in denial about situations and relationships in our lives that need repair. For example, in feigning naiveté or lack of knowledge regarding the scarcity of genuine sisterhood, we are, in fact, denying the existence of unsisterly behavior. This often occurs when we either pretend that something exists that doesn't or when we focus more on the ideal, rather than expose adversarial behavior in hopes of eradicating it. Calling attention to the destructive, self-destructive, and inauthentic behavior might very well command its demise. Given that we know all too well how comforting sisterhood is, we must welcome it and its rewards for others as well as for ourselves. Thus, for the moment, let us reflect on how much more beautiful our world would be if all sisters simply loved each another. Our children would be more secure, for they would have not just one female guardian, but many to attend to their everyday needs. As the ancient African proverb goes, "It takes a village to raise a child," a truism that former First Lady Hillary Rodham Clinton observed in her much celebrated and frequently quoted 1996 title, *It Takes a Village*, which remained on the Best Sellers list for twenty weeks that year. As for our men, they, too, would be better partners in our male-female relationships, understanding now the true power of sisterhood and, more importantly, understanding and acknowledging the role that they themselves play in bringing about and perpetuating unsisterly conduct. Once women "get themselves together," their male counterparts would have little choice but to follow. For example, women could no longer be pitted against each other, with the result that, both physically and emotionally abusive male-female relationships would decline significantly, with the realization that women are now in support of each other rather than in opposition. Their support of each other would aid in uplifting their self-esteem, indeed, a necessary ingredient in their refusal to be physically and/or emotionally disrespected by their male companions. With this needed support system in place, women would be better able to rise up against all forms of abuse related to incidences of the battered female by her male counterpart. In the end, men would truly learn to respect the institution and constitution of womanhood and sisterhood, as they would respect our refusal to compete for their companionship while sacrificing our true selves and/or betraying sisterly love. Since many solid female relationships are broken when competition and betrayal (.e.g, physical attraction to the male counterpart and/or adultery) move in, we would witness a shift in this phenomenon as our attitudes towards each other shift. If we but forestall such temptations, the world would be a better place for all humankind; all would be able to embrace and enjoy true respect, self-esteem, love, and happiness. Sisterhood, indeed, undergirds the Africana family, thereby establishing our collective role in society.

What we obviously fail to understand is that we are participating in a vicious cycle of misery and doom, for one cannot expect love and happiness without first offering those things to the universe. When I speak in terms of the universe, I am speaking of substantive things, for instance an individual occupying positive space. Why not share that warm experience with another sister? Here again Morrison says it well:

> *In your rainbow journey toward the realization of personal goals, don't make choices based only on your security and your safety. Nothing is safe. . . . But in pursuing your highest ambitions, don't let your personal safety diminish the safety of your stepsister. In wielding the power that is deservedly yours, don't permit it to enslave your stepsisters. Let your might and your power emanate from that place in you that is nurturing and caring." ["Cinderella's Stepsisters", 83-4]*

Further, to paraphrase the old saying, we are our sisters' keepers. Let me, then, suggest that we take one simple but giant step in reversing this vicious and self-destructive cycle. Whenever you find yourself emitting negative rather than positive energy, you must just stop and ask yourself one question. Does this benefit me or anyone else for that matter? Better still, would it not be better to play a positive role, helping someone realize happiness rather than contributing to that person's grief? If for no reason other than just doing it for yourself, remember that the world does operate on an echo system. What you put out inevitably comes back and returns twofold, threefold, or even more in other ways. Would it not then be better for you to receive multiple successes and blessings rather than multiply failures and misfortunes? The question is rhetorical, of course. But, unless you are self-destructive, you would most likely prefer, justifiably so, to join the community of complete, well-rounded, loving sisters, as described in Mona Lake Jones' colorful poem, "A Room Full of Sisters":

> *A room full of sisters, like jewels in a crown*
> *Vanilla, cinnamon, and dark chocolate brown . . .*

> *Now picture yourself in the midst of this glory*
> *As I describe the sisters who were part of this story.*

> *They were wearing purple, royal blues and all shades of reds*
> *Some had elegant hats on their heads.*

> *With sparkling eyes and shinny lips*
> *They moved through the room swaying their hips.*

> *Speaking with smiles on their African faces*
> *Their joy and laughter filled all the spaces.*

> *They were fashionable and stylish in what they were wearing*
> *Kind sisters who were loving and caring.*

> *You see, it's not about how these sisters appeared*
> *Their beauty was in the value they revered.*

> *They were smart, articulate and well read*
> *With all kinds of Black history stored in their heads.*

Jugglers of profession, managers of lives
Mothers of children, lovers and wives.

Good-hearten reaching out to others
Giving back to the community and supporting our brothers.

All of these sisters struggled the past
Suffered from prejudice, endured the wrath.

But they brushed off their dresses and pushed on the door
And they came back stronger than they were before.

Now, imagine if you will
The essence and thrill

As you stand feeling proud
In the heart of this crowd

Sisterhood of modern Sojourners today
Still out in front blazing the way.

A room full of sisters, like jewels in a crown
Vanilla, cinnamon, and dark chocolate brown.
(From The Color of Culture)

To be sure, this poem, which presents a dramatic commentary on the beauty of genuine sisterhood, explores the richness, the power, and the pure pleasure of a rare and wholesome bonding among sisters. It anticipates the joy of reciprocal sisterly acts, while making possible the common reality of sisterhood. It is a relationship that allows participants to share their sacred and innermost thoughts, to confide in each other, and in so doing, lay bare one's most intimate and often times joyous experiences. Thus, each gives and receives mutual support in standing up on behalf of the other and, by extension on behalf of, our entire Africana community. Such is the way it must be among Africana women if true success, peace, and harmony are to reign.

(Reprint, Chapter V, *Africana Womanist Literary Theory*, 2004, 65-77)

BIBLIOGRAPHY

Andrews, Larry R. "Black Sisterhood in Gloria Naylor's Novels." *CLA Journal*, September 1989.

Bâ, Mariama. *So Long a Letter*. Great Britain: Heinemann, 1989.

Clinton, Hillary Rodham. *It Takes a Village: And Other Lessons Children Teach Us*. New York: Simon and Schuster, 1996.

Hudson-Weems, Clenora. *Africana Womanism: Reclaiming Ourselves*. Troy, Mich: Bedford Publishers, 1993.

Hurston, Zora Neale. *Their Eyes Were Watching God*. Urbana, Ill: University of Illinois Press, 1978.

Jones, Mona Lake. "A Room Full of Sisters" In *The Color of Culture*. Seattle, Wash: Impact Communications, 1993.

Morrison, Toni. "Cinderella's Stepsisters." In *Issues Across the Curriculum : Reading, Writing, Research*. Edited by Delores LaGuardia and Hans Guth. Mountain View, Calif: Mayfield Publishing, 1997. pp 282-284.

_____*Sula*. New York: Bantam Books, 1973.

Naylor, Gloria. *Mama Day*. New York: Vintage Books, 1989.

Shakespeare, William. *Othello* 3.3.165-67. *The Riverside Shakespeare*, 2nd ed. Boston: Houghton Mifflin, 1997.

Sofola, 'Zula. Foreword to *Africana Womanism: Reclaiming Ourselves*. Troy, Mich: Bedford Publishers, 1993.

Villarosa, Linda. "Circles of Sisterhood." *Essence*, October 1994; 81-86.

Chapter Six

Africana Male-Female Relationships and Sexism in the Community

I remain persuaded of the inevitable and necessary complementarity of man and woman.

Love, imperfect as it may be in its content and expression, remains the natural link between these two beings.

To love one another! If only each partner could move sincerely towards the other! If each could only melt into the other! If each would only accept the other's successes and failures! If each would only praise the other's qualities instead of listing his faults! If each could only correct bad habits without harping on about them! If each could penetrate the other's most secret haunts to forestall failure and be a support while tending to the evils that are repressed!

The success of the family is born of a couple's harmony, as the harmony of multiple instruments creates a pleasant symphony.

The nation is made up of all the families, rich or poor, united or separated, aware or unaware. The success of a nation therefore depends inevitably on the family (Bâ 88-89).

The above quotation is from the Senegalese novel, *So Long a Letter*, by Miarama Ba. The protagonist, Ramatoulaye, offers excellent pointers concerning love and marriage. In her reflections on her marriage, the advice she gives represents the ideal in male-female relationships, which unfortunately she was unable to experience, not necessarily because of any identifiable faults of her own, but rather because of the decisions her husband Modou makes about marriage and commitment, based, for the most part, upon the external forces and practices of legalized polygamy in the Islamic communities of Senagal. Thus, Ramatoulaye contends that, in her country, "all women have almost the same fate, which religions or unjust legislation have sealed" (88).

Shifting from the continent of Africa to America, the subject of Africana male-female relationships remains a much-discussed issue. Attempts to reassess these relationships command an engagement in historicizing circumstances of Africana people, which includes not only focusing on the matter of the personal love between a couple, but also considering the impact of the social, political, economic, and cultural milieu on the total Africana family as well. The following quotation comments on the history of Africana male-female relationships in America based upon a support system in the face of racial adversity, an Africana womanist priority that has been replaced today with women's issues, many of them, unfortunately by Black women:

> *Until the 1950s, strong relationships existed between black women and black men. They were the major factor in keeping racism from destroying the black family and the black community in America. Now, it has been replaced, in many instances, by a war between genders—a war in which there can be no winners.. The real casualties will be the black families and black children of America. [Reynolds, Do Black Women Hate Black Men? xi]*

The searing fifties and sixties ushered in two significant, politicized phenomena: The first was the advent of the inception of the modern civil rights movement ignited by the brutal lynching of Emmett Louis "Bobo" Till, a fourteen-year-old Black Chicago youth, for whistling at a twenty-one-year old white woman, in Money, Mississippi, on 28 August, 1955. This horrific incident occurred just three months prior to Rosa Parks' refusal to relinquish her bus seat to a white man in Montgomery, Alabama, 1 December, 1955. The second, culminating in the sixties, was the rise in popularity of avenues or places for women in society, accurately characterizing the age of the woman, which brought forth the women's liberation movement, led by Betty Friedan, one of the shapers of modern day feminism, and the author of *The Feminist Mystique*. With this new emphasis on women and gender issues came an increased de-emphasis on the black liberation struggle. This new wave of feminism had a decidedly negative impact on the Africana community, particularly on the Africana family with regard to its male-female relationships, the very foundation of positive Africana life. But that is not the only threatening force in the black community. Sexism, too, plays its part in dividing our community, as this menacing factor wreaks havoc on the sanctity and harmony of the Africana family. Thus, with the weight of racial oppression and diabolical pressures still omnipresent since the involuntary migration and arrival of Africans to this continent, along with the patriarchal system of sexism and female subjugation, strained relations between Africana men and women have become a salient phenomenon in the Africana community.

For centuries, Africana men and women have been forging a collective battle against racist oppression in America. This two-prong support system, the male-female collective struggle, which is one of the eighteen descriptors for Africana Womanism, has proven to be the most effective in combating racism. Africana Womanism, which insists upon this mutual respect and inclusivity, strives to break the gender barriers between the Africana man and woman. It becomes clear, then, that while the most devastating threat to our community remains racism, some serious attention must also be given to Africana male-female relationships, wherein lies the survival of the Africana family and, by extension, the entire Africana community. To be sure, strong bonds between Africana couples must be established in order that the black liberation struggle be strengthened and therefore empowered. According to black arts poet and critic Haki R. Madhubuti, who takes the political stance of the interlocutory nature of black male-female relationships and the on going black liberation struggle:

> *Black couples must understand that "Black love" in the United States is much more than a commitment between two people; it is also the realization that there are political, economic, historical, racial, familial, and emotional forces impacting upon that loveship. [Madhubuti, Black Men 180]*

101

Further, he asserts:

The root as well as the quality of Black life is in the relationship established between Black men and women in a white supremacist system. Black struggle, that is, the liberation of our people, starts in the home. [Madhubuti 60]

Given such contentions by one of our most unrelenting Black culturalist and liberation advocates since the sixties, a period that has been historically characterized as an all-time high point of the black liberation struggle, it becomes critical that the personal relationship between the Africana couple be perfected if the family unit constituting the over-all Africana community is to survive. Moreover, Madhubuti's assessment here accurately identifies the controlling ingredients necessary for a long-lasting, positive Africana male-female relationship, one that includes not only emotional and physical components, but historical, political, and economical dynamics as well. Necessarily, the Africana male-female relationship requires a unified commitment from both parties, a commitment they share for the benefit of their personal and communal fulfillment. The focus on the complexity of the Africana community, then, emulating from the love between Africana men and women, sets forth the parameters for analyzing the dynamics of Africana male-female relationships and for establishing plausible strategies to make them work.

Because many Africana women have shifted their allegiance from the struggle against racial oppression to the struggle against gender oppression in the midst of the women's era, Africana men have begun to feel alienated, believing that their female counterparts are abandoning them and the liberation struggle, a belief that, no doubt has some merit. Understanding that the primary concern for the feminist is female empowerment rather than race empowerment, their feelings of betrayal, frustration, abandonment, and the likes are natural. Some may even call it paranoia on the part of the Africana man, but whatever one calls it, it exists. Sociologist Dolores Aldridge comments on this element of betrayal in *Focusing: Black Male-Female Relationships* (35). With this in mind, it must be noted that in the final analysis, when those Africana women finish fighting the feminist battle and feminists have succeeded in realizing all their goals relative to female empowerment, the Africana woman will be left with the reality that she is both black and at the bottom. Such was the case with the June 1995 Supreme Court ruling on the unconstitutionality of Affirmative Action Set Asides that were racially based. Those based on gender equality were found constitutionally sound but the black woman remains classified as black first. Hence, the Africana woman, after a lengthy absence from the black liberation struggle, will then find herself coming back to her male counterpart and to her community to pick up the on going liberation struggle for her entire family.

The threat of the female-centered, female-empowerment ideology of feminism undoubtedly has begun to diminish the significance of the traditional family-centered, race-empowerment philosophy of the black liberation movement. Refocusing this political orientation of the Africana woman, in conjunction with her family, has resulted in weakening the Africana community. In Contrast, operating within the constructs of an Africana womanist paradigm, then, re-shifts the focus away from race myopic feminism to African-centered solutions to the breakdown in Africana male- female relationships. Such solutions are grounded in three key interconnecting components—the centrality of family, the love for each other, and the commitment to the liberation struggle for ultimate survival. Needless to say, viewing the problems through the paradigm of Africana Womanism in order to bring about total parity for Africana men and women in a racist society must now identify the critical issues impeding their progress.

Africana Womanism, necessarily must first contend with the disharmony within the Africana family, that pervades and penetrates all aspects of the lives of Africana men and women, especially their personal/love relationships. Disharmony, which is frequently the result of financial hardships, lack of commitment to each other and to the overall Africana community, and the lack of trust and communication are inextricably linked to our emotional strife. What this suggests, then, is that rather than taking an oppositional posture in reaction to perceived irresolvable differences between men and women, Africana Womanism instead highlights a structure wherein Africana women work with Africana men in dissolving both the sense of alienation that

Africana men experience and the sense of isolation and suppression that Africana women experience.

In the case of the Africana male, participation in all aspects of the culture is encouraged. For example, he, as is the case of the woman, is charged with the responsibilities of accepting his shortcomings/limitations and acknowledging them in a sharing attempt to redirect the outcome. Expounding on this reciprocal nature of positive male-female relationships, Madhubuti asserts that The African American man must always listen to his partner, the black man must also be able to reciprocate. He must involve himself in all aspects of housework. He must involve himself in the birth of his children. He must always accept the blame for his own imperfections and try to change for the better (181-183). With these mandates for positive relationships come genuine caring and compassion, both of which foster a positive dependency of one upon the other. It should be noted here that needing one another is not a negative practice; thus, there is no need to apologize for needing each other's love and presence. Only when one can admit to and appreciate this interdependency can a relationship truly grow into something beautiful and permanent. As stated in *Africana Womanism*,

> *Positive male companionship is of great interest to the Africana womanist in general, for she realizes that male and female relationships are not only comforting but the key to perpetuating the human race. Without each other, the human race becomes extinct. The Africana womanist also realizes that, while she loves and respects herself and is, in general, at peace with herself, she ultimately desires a special somebody to fill a void in her life, one who makes her complete. [Hudson-Weems 67]*

Na'im Akbar expounded on this concept in his 1989 contribution "Materialism and Chauvinism," where he concludes:

> *African American men and women must not fall victim to the expanding unisexualism so prevalent in American society. They must preserve the uniqueness of their separate, complementary roles. They must also avoid ontological weakness which equates nurturance, dependence, dependence and supportiveness with*

weakness. They must also avoid the highly destructive macho notions of manhood which are feverishly trying to be realized by both men and women in their striving for a faulty liberation (55).

Clearly, a realization of Africana womanist goals for a harmonious Africana male-female relationship demands reincorporation of the Africana male from his position of alienation from his family and community to a cooperative center with the strength of his female counterpart. It is equally important that each partner have realistic expectations in a relationship rather than unrealistic demands, that may only end in disappointments, thereby ultimately destroying an otherwise healthy relationship. For example, idealistically women often desire tall, clean cut, educated men with high income. They want it all. Many men, too, though many are often intimidated by their success, want it all, preferring women who are both beautiful and successful. The truth of the matter is that both should be focusing on what each could contribute to a healthy relationship, rather than on selfish needs.

In this regard, the lines of communication are blurred, which prohibits the existence of any true positive male-female relationship. It is here that one can truly open up one's feelings, expressing one's needs and desires, as well as confessing and admitting one's shortcomings and mistakes. The two magic words—"I'm sorry"—are key to a positive male-female relationship, as they can begin the healing process for a troubled relationship. Admitting fault usually leads to forgiveness. Such communication and commitment without fear, wherein both parents listen to each other as a means of sharing, which promotes bonding, indeed, fosters positive male-female relationships.

On the subject of commitment, Staples has the paralleling theories of Black women and men. For the former, he feels that "some have a fear of making a commitment and suffering the fate of many black women being rejected and winding up as a divorcee with children to support" (Staples 78). Such fear generating from women is due large in part to their being products of broken homes. For men, Staple contends that "Due to the black man's desire to maintain control of his situation and his image of masculinity, refusal to make a commitment is one way of achieving the power balance in a relationship" (Staples 79). Further there is the issue of leaving the solution to the problem for the women to handle, which they do often times without the male input. This may be because, as Staple surmises, "The excess number of black women in the eligible pool and the concentration of so many educated, attractive women and their implicit sexual and emotional demands may overwhelm them. With so many women to choose from it becomes more difficult for black men to form committed relationships" (Staples 77). Finally, the over abundance of female choices distracts from the need to commit on the part of Black men.

In this respect, there is little room, if any, for selfishness. The goal, then, becomes what is good for the whole, i.e. for the family, rather than what is in it for the self. Of course, there are problems of financial support and the lack of sufficient, not excessive, funds, which often result, in some instances, in a lack of mutual respect and even in low self-esteem. However, if the relationship has more fun and lightheartedness, that is, laughter that the joy of true friendship can create, it is easier to cope with financial shortcomings. Indeed, if there is no relief, there is little hope for a relationship laden with boredom, complaints, and unrelenting gravity, compounded by the problem of limited funds. Not surprisingly, what we witness with the Africana man, much like the Africana woman, is his heretofore unacknowledged tripartite plight—race, class, and gender; that is, long-standing traditional male roles dictated by a white, racist, patriarchal system, that makes unrealistic demands on Africana men, who have historically been disenfranchised.

> *Africana men, too, [like the Africana woman] have not had the consistent experience of upholding the traditional role of the male as the head of the household. In a traditional patriarchal system the male is expected to fulfill the responsibilities outside the home, such as earning money, while serving as the official head inside the home. On the home base, he dictates the order of the household and designates the woman to carry it out. [Hudson-Weems 64]*

This particularly contentious issue within Africana families with the male as breadwinner is particularly problematic, as his lack of resources has often rendered him impotent in earning sufficient wages to defray

106

household expenses without the assistance of his female counterpart. In fact, the often-touted two-family income, a marker of progressive modern evolution of the family structure, is in reality a necessity for the Africana family. Paradoxically, in the society we live in, it is also an indicator of the inferior status of the Africana male and the devolution of the Africana family structure. Given this heavy gender burden based upon a class system in which capital in unequally distributed, the economic predicament of the Africana male represents one of the most complex dilemmas facing Africana male-female relationships. Nathan Hare, in *Crisis in Black Sexual Politics* suggests a positive response to the financial predicament of Africana men and women in the following quotation:

> *The young Black woman will do well to be supportive of her man while remaining firm in her rights, understanding while not necessarily condoning her mate's hesitation in the face of unfair adversity. Rather than chastise her man, however, for his mediocre occupation, she might better find something good to say while remaining alert to signs of simmering ambition on his part as a basis for further encouragement on hers [125].*

Such a situation breeds another monster--drug or alcohol abuse, ultimately erupting into domestic violence as a means of escape and pressure release. This harsh scenario is exemplified in the underlying theme of Terry McMillan's *Disappearing Acts*: The Africana man is trapped within a patriarchal model and its attendant abuses. This narrative of the almost insurmountable challenges and the unconquerable spirit of black love is demonstrated in the frustrating predicament of the two protagonists, Zora and Franklin. Though ultimately they overcome such potentially debilitating and life-threatening illnesses as drug and alcohol abuse and epilepsy, this Africana couple provides an encouraging model, for the two real health problems facing each individual draw attention to the need for Africana people to collectively encounter and successfully navigate through communal and professional resources for healing and recovering from our physical and emotional illnesses. Hence, there is no way to have a wholesome relationship if one is not in control of one's faculties, which have been altered by the intrusion of alien agencies. Such control can be neither recovered nor maintained in a state of "selfish" individualism. That said, it must be added that as literature reflects reality, much truth emerges from fiction. Such is the case of *Disappearing Acts*.

As a novel whose characters are committed to a positive male-female relationship and making it work, *Disappearing Acts* abounds in the Africana womanist characteristic of being in concert with the male counterpart in the struggle. In it, Franklin is the product of the "last hired, first fired syndrome," which is a direct result of racism. In spite of everything, Zora does not consider his inability to maintain employment a reflection of his manhood or of any lack thereof. Although Franklin's pride makes it difficult for him to accept her constant financial support, she sticks by him, even making some personal sacrifices in the process.

> *Franklin. Didn't I make you float? Didn't I give you spring in winter? Didn't I show you rainbows and everything else that moved inside me? I gave birth to you child because I loved you. I stuck by you when you were broke, because I loved you. I stuck by you for everything, because I loved you. So tell me, goddammit, wasn't that enough? [McMillan 366]*

Of course, this tirade comes after Zora is forced to have Franklin removed from their apartment because of physical violence and its continuing threat. Even so, in doing this, she is, in fact, loving herself and her child enough to grant him the space he needs to recover, which he ultimately does. "It takes a lot for Zora to come to this decision, but she realizes that this is the only way Franklin can save himself and their relationship. He has to redeem himself. She is not able to do it for him, although she has tried too many times before" (Hudson-Weems 140). Fortunately for this family unit, in the end there is hope for them, although this is not always the case in our communities.

Ironically, both the core of declining Africana male and female relationships and its solutions lie predominately in three critical issues: (i) reciprocal appreciation of each other, which Maulana Karenga defines as a "positive sharing and its mutual investment in each other's happiness, well-being and development"; (ii) the politics of economics, as outlined above in the triple plight of Africana men and women; and (iii) the establishment of an authentic value system that promotes a collective liberation struggle which compliments personal relationships. Along these lines, Karenga cites black sociologists Joyce Ladner and Robert Staples, who argue for "the need for a value system which rejects and counters the standards of the dominant society" (Karenga 295). This is the very "value system" manifested in the paradigmatic structure of Africana Womanism, for too many Africanans have brought European cultural values and perspectives to their relationships. According to Belle, Bouie, and Baldwin:

> *African Americans continue to negotiate their survival in a society where the major institutions are governed by the principles and values of the Euro-American worldview. Having existed in a Eurocentric social reality over several centuries, evidence suggests that African Americans have become psychologically dependent, in varying degrees, on that reality. Consequently, they have accepted an orientation to social relationships, which is more consistent in many respects with Eurocentric cultural definitions than with their own Afrocentric cultural definitions. This state of psychological oppression means that many African American males and females have internalized Eurocentric definitions/values and practice them in their relationships. [50-51]*

Karenga's identification of the four basic connections (cash, flesh, force, and dependency), expounds on problems in Africana male-female relationships that are informed by this inauthentic value system for blacks. In erroneously assuming that money is the solution to all problems, and that, in fact, it buys whatever is desired, including your partner, we find ourselves slipping into a commercial, materialistic mode of thinking, reflective of a value system created by Western culture. To be sure, this is an inauthentic behavior pattern relative to an Africana perspective that needs correcting. This is not to say that we do not need finances to survive; however, extravagance and over abundance are not parts of the real equation for the lives of authentic Africana people. Admittedly, finances play a large part in the security of relationships, and thus, while it is difficult to acknowledge, when finances fall into trouble, relationships, too, fall into trouble. It is evident that a relationship does not exist in a vacuum, and thus, the couple's financial stability invariably affects how they interact on all fronts. When we find ourselves in a financial bind, i.e. when bills cannot be paid, when necessities cannot be met, we subsequently find ourselves in a stressful mode, operating under the stressful circumstances of financial strife and depravation. Unfortunately, this reality is all to often the case with Africana couples who sadly enough are often the victims of racial discrimination.

The old scenario "last hired, first fired" has much validity for Susan Ferguson so aptly puts it, "when the ax falls, [blacks] usually have even fewer resources than whites to help them through the tough times" (Ferguson 533). This is certainly not to suggest that every circumstance regarding financial hardships is a matter of racism. We cannot, however, deny the frequency of its occurrence either, for it's victimization does not stop there. It insinuates itself into every personal corner of one's existence, into our private relationships and intimate places. No matter how hard we fight it, we cannot feign peace and happiness when we are unable to meet everyday necessities that depend upon solvency. We may swoon into infidelity or even find ourselves saying unkind things to each other, with an overwhelming air of impatience and venom, as if our partner is at all times the culprit in this unwelcome and unpleasant situation. Sadly, the saying "no money, no honey," which rings true to some degree, is illustrative of the tremendous breakdown in mutual respect between Africana men and women. Clearly, both partners have to remember that rules governing human relationships are not necessarily applicable to financial ones. Successful male-female relationships operate within a core realm of mutual respect and love for one another. The Africana man must understand and appreciate his female counterpart. He must respect her as mother, culture bearer, and co-partner. To disrespect her is to disrespect self. Likewise, the Africana woman must realize that the Africana man is father, protector, and co-partner. As such, he, too, is deserving of reciprocal love and respect. Simply put, there must be reciprocal love and respect for one another before a lasting wholesome relationship can truly exist.

For Africana people, there is also the element of confusion in prioritizing that leads to a tendency of appropriating someone else's agenda, reflecting someone else's particular priorities. As an African people, we come from a collective and family-centered perspective, with emphasis on the intertwined nature of our destiny as a whole. With that in mind, then, the question of the feminist agenda comes to the forefront as to whether it is taking its toll on today's Africana community. Does it negatively impact upon Africana male-female relationships? Can feminist language and attitudes, which some find problematic largely because of some strong anti-male overtones, work in the home place as well as in the work place for Africana people? And finally, are there options relative to creating positive Africana male-female relationships, the foundation of an ideal family structure, in order to ensure a more holistic life for all? Indeed, these critical questions are at the crux of the matter in instigating the breakdown in positive Africana male-female relationships. Without positive interdependence and interrelationship between the sexes, including the creation of our own authentic language as a means of communicating and defining our authentic activities and existence as an Africana people, positive male-female relationships will not be possible, which translates into the ultimate extinction of Africana families/communities.

As Africana Womanism proposes eighteen distinct features characterizing the Africana woman, it proposes the same features for the male counterpart. Both are self-namers, self-definers, family-centered, in concert with their counterparts in the liberation struggle; flexible role players, strong, ambitious, respectful of elders, whole, and authentic. Additionally, the true Africana man is female compatible, moral, role model, supportive, respectful of women, protecting, fathering, and loving. Both parties evince the salient elements of spirituality and morality. It is important to understand that recognition of and respect for the existence of a higher power, which guides personal and social behavior and thus prohibits immoral acts like infidelity, perversion, etc., are the penultimate qualities of any positive and complete male-female relationship. In other words, without a spiritual presence in our lives, all else is null and void. Moreover, if both men and women aspire to perfecting themselves by adopting these qualities in their lives, they would then find the kind of mutual love, respect, and support that could only lead to an ideal spirit-guided relationship between the two. It is crucial, then, for Africana men and women to work diligently toward tailoring their own agenda, so that their needs and concerns may be more accurately and expediently addressed. This includes the specific problems of the Africana woman today, particularly as some have unsuccessfully tried to address their needs through a feminist construct or paradigm. In this regard, the lines of common action are blurred, prohibiting the existence of any true positive black male-female relationship. It is here that the couple can truly open up their hearts, expressing their needs and desires, as well as confessing and admitting their shortcomings and mistakes. "I am sorry," the three magic words that are key to positive male-female relationships, can begin the healing process for a troubled relationship. To be sure, admitting fault usually leads to forgiveness. Such common action and commitment without fear, wherein each partner listens to the other as a means of sharing, ultimately promote the kind of bonding necessary for making positive male-female relationships.

On the subject of commitment, Robert Staples has paralleling theories for both women and men. For the former, he believes that "Some have a fear of making a commitment and suffering the fate of many black women [that is] being rejected and winding up as a divorcee with children to support" (Staples, 78). Such fear generating from women is for the most part because they are products of broken homes. For the latter, he contends that "because of the Black man's desire to maintain control of his situation, and his image of masculinity, refusal to make a commitment is one way of achieving the power balance in a relationship" (Staples, 79). Insecurity makes him fear that the woman may dictate the nature of the relationship and take control of its destiny. In avoiding ties, he escapes this dreaded possibility. Of course, all too frequently there is the issue of consciously relegating problem solving to women, which they often do without male input. Moreover, the "excess number of Black women in the eligible pool and the concentration of so many educated, attractive women and their implicit sexual and emotional demands may overwhelm them. With so many women to choose from it becomes more difficult for Black men to form committed relationships" (Staples, 77). Unquestionably, the over abundance of female choices distracts from the need of many Black men to make commitments.

Continuing with the focus on habits prohibiting positive Africana male-female relations, there is the issue of the wide-spread incarceration of Africana men, which is a rapidly growing phenomenon. Many studies examine the racist aspect of the pervasive incriminization process of Africana men. According to one source, "When African-Americans are subjected to trial, they [Africana men] are often given especially harsh sentences" (Miller 76). With this kind of sentencing comes a decline in employment, for criminal records often have a direct connection to unemployment. The problem is indeed mind-boggling. We can only hope that someone will soon introduce a means of truly exposing this unjust practice, thereby breaking this vicious cycle that impacts negatively on the Africana family. Moreover, there is the problem of womanizing, whoring [as in the case of the woman], selfishness, homosexuality, and bisexuality, all of which play a large role in the breakdown in Africana male-female relations. Womanizing and whoring, remain critical and legitimate concerns for many men and women today, as many of them desire monogamous relationships, two of the most crucial ones: love, and fear of contacting fatal diseases. In the case of the male, perhaps because of the "male shortage," many men believe they should have "carte blanche" regarding the number of women they should have, with no questions asked. Unfortunately, having several women does not necessarily guarantee true love or happiness, which is why so many men are still of the opinion that it really only takes the right person to make one really and truly happy.

The matter of selfishness is another big problem in Africana male-female relationships. While it is difficult to pinpoint just where this propensity originates, I am of the opinion that women, as culture bearers, mothers and nurturers, three of the eighteen characteristics of Africana Womanism - we are in many ways responsible for rearing these generations of selfish beings, individuals who almost always make their decisions based on what they themselves want or need, rather than on what is most beneficial to the family. While it is not always the case, women on the whole, are more inclined to family-centered decisions. In any event, the only recourse for survival of the Africana male-female relationship is to grow up and put an end to selfishness, thereby putting the family first for a change.

On a final note, sexism in the Africana community is an issue that we cannot take lightly. The late Audre Lourde, Africana literary critic and poet, makes the following assessment of the racism and sexism in the Africana community:

> *Black women's literature is full of the pain of frequent assault, not only by racist patriarchy, but also by Black men. Yet the necessity for and history of shared battle have made us, Black women, particularly vulnerable to the false accusation that anti-sexist is anti-Black. Meanwhile, woman hating as a recourse of the powerless is sapping strength from Black communities and our very lives. [Lourde, "Age, Race, Class, and Sex," 356]*

The fact remains that while the number one obstacle to success for Africana people is racism, the problem of sexism in our community continues to rear its ugly head, with the full knowledge that this problem is not only inauthentic but, more importantly, unfeasible since we are, after all, in a collective struggle for the survival of our entire family - men, women, and children. This is not to say that the Africana woman does not desire total equality with her male counterpart. Quite the contrary, for egalitarianism has always been a key factor in the Africana family, and as equal partners, we must insist upon that status. Granted, there are some real indications of female subjugation in the Africana community, a clear case of black man duplicating the white man's tactics, which are rooted in racism. According to Maulana Karenga,

> *Racism engenders self-hate, self-doubt and pathological fixation on the white paradigm. And sexism encourages artificial personal power over women as a substitute for real social power over one's destiny and daily life (Introduction to Black Studies 292).*

For the Africana man there is obviously serious confusion about his logic in regard to power. Believing that oppressing women represents power is absurd, for when he goes beyond that point, the Africana man will still be left with a tremendous sense of powerlessness as to how society regards him, an image that is unaltered and unaffected in any positive sense by his mistreatment of his female counterpart. Consequently, this behavior is counterproductive and hence cannot be tolerated; it must be banned from our community forever. Moreover, we need only scratch the surface to conclude that any thinking person can see through that pose and understand that the Africana man has absolutely no institutionalized power to oppress Africana women, or anybody else for that matter, to the same degree as white men have regarding their women and people in general. Hence, there is no need for the same kind of antagonism between Africana men and women that exists between white men and women. There is only a need for renegotiation and for clarity about the fact that we are indeed equals and equally oppressed by a racist system.

While it is obvious that men generally have more physical prowess than women, their tendency towards verbal and/or physical abuse of their female counterparts should not be interpreted as a birthright. In futilely seeking their manhood in the subjugation of black women, Africana men fail to understand that they and their female counterparts are inextricably bound together as equals. The problem is that they are unaware of the true source of their pain, an unrelenting torment they find almost impossible to articulate. The result is their expression of internal struggle superficially alleviated by violence not only towards each other, as manifested in gang violence and drug abuse; but towards women in particular, as manifested in female bashing. In spite of their natural inclination to feel a connection with their women, who complete their sense of being, feeling the brunt of the white man's oppression makes them both vulnerable and sensitive, which is nonetheless manifested by a pose of insensitive behavior. Therefore, they find themselves in the peculiar predicament of hurting the very ones who are "in their corner." Rather than seek vindication for their feelings of frustration and inadequacy on their female counterparts, they would be better to hold the true culprit responsible, perhaps the initial but essential step in helping to eradicate sexism in our community. Moreover, because of economic stresses, high unemployment and low wages, minimum education and illiteracy, for example - Africana men have again taken out their frustrations on their women, oftentimes envying the financial achievements that some Africana women have gained over them. Cyclical in nature, this anger and frustration continue to feed upon themselves. In the final analysis, however, muscle flexing can never translate into having true power, and the sooner Africana men realize this, the sooner we can go on about the business of pursuing what Vivian Gordon calls "the partnership struggle with black men [and black women] for the emancipation of their communities" (Gordon 13). To be sure, Africana men need both their women and their communities at the center of their lives in order to become whole and complete, which could ultimately heal the history of abuse and female subjugation. Because the lives and destinies of Africana men and women are so interconnected, their psychics need to be healed together, facilitating proper nurturing for the survival of our communities and our children, our future.

Because a large part of sexist behavior is societal, it is fairly difficult for men in general to avoid being sexist to some degree. This is because of the way we are taught and trained and the roles men and women are assigned in society. Men continue to hold the most powerful positions in society. The Africana man mimics white society; yet, his racially based limitations complicate his position, thereby constantly challenging his masculinity. As a consequence, the Africana man, feeling that within his home, one of the few places where he can assert his masculine authority without retribution, he can exert his masculinity, his sense of power over his female counterpart. Needless to say, sexism in the black community, which is a contradiction to our historical reality, must be addressed.

Unlike whites, Africana men and women have been equals from the beginning, as we originated from the continent of Africa, an agricultural land where equal sharing of responsibilities and status is mandatory. This is not to suggest that female subjugation does not currently exist in Africa, for it does. While some levels of oppression of women predate the advent of colonialism in Africa, it was not the kind of exploitative oppression we speak of in terms of female subjugation today. Then, men were conscientious and therefore pledge their commitment to the community. Today sexism in the African family represents a form of European structural duplication. The idea of egalitarianism within the Africana family does not suggest that there are no male and female roles, for there are, indeed, defined roles in our society. What must be made clear, of course, is that the roles in the Africana family are necessarily flexible, as is the case of the Africana woman as flexible role player. Thus, one role is no less important than another. While sexism may not be totally eradicated within the near future, one can make a conscious effort on a daily basis to correct it. Moreover, our community, like the Africana woman, must prioritize our battles so that the most threatening one to our families and to our communities will have first priority in order to ensure black survival. It is clear that we have our own way of looking at things and of putting those things into proper perspective via prioritization. This does not compromise or lessen the seriousness of sexism nor the need for eradicating this phenomenon, which has penetrated our world and violated our personal lives. Thus, in much the same way that we address the triple plight of Africana women from an Africana womanist perspective, i.e., prioritizing race, class, and gender, while dismissing none of the blows to our existence, we must likewise prioritize our attack on all forms of oppression within the Africana community, including the inauthentic and menacing problem of female subjugation. To be sure, the eradication of this obstacle to the over-all well-being of the Africana family and community would, indeed, lift us to a higher level of harmony and collective struggle, which is necessary to carry us into this new millennium successfully.

As is evident, a Eurocentric blueprint for positive Africana male-female relationships is unrealistic, as "Black male-female relationships, which prioritize Eurocentric values seemingly, would be less stable than Black heterosexual relationships with a stronger Afrocentric cultural foundation; (Belle, Bouie, and Baldwin 52). We must understand that we, Africana men and women, are in this together. We need to recognize that we are each other's better half, and that we need each other in order to work through this crisis. We need to understand that, contrary to some beliefs, we are not each other's enemy, and that, at times, when our self-esteem is at its lowest, when racism has dealt a low blow to both our psyche and our pocketbook, we need to reach out to one another, giving all the love and understanding possible in order for us to evolve as positive beings. True, there may be times when we strike out against that which is closest to us in our moments of frustration and despair, but we must redirect that negative energy, transferring it into some positive soul love for each other, realizing that we need each other now as always and even more than ever today. Hence, Africana men and women, working together, represent the only way the global African community can be rejuvenated. Only then can our personal lives be somewhat restored to a state of harmony, security, and happiness enabling us to move positively to a higher level of existence, free of racism, classism, and sexism.

The person I love will strengthen me by endorsing my assumption of my manhood [womanhood], while the need to

117

earn the admiration or the love of other will erect a value-making superstructure on my whole vision of the world. {Fanon 41)

SUMMATION LIST OF 15 POSITIVE/NEGATIVE ELEMENTS OF MALE/FEMALE RELATIONSHIPS

Positive Negative

Positive	Negative
1.Love	1. Contempt
2. Friendship	2. Rivalry
3.Trust	3. Distrust
4.Fidelity	4. Infidelity
5.Truth	5. Deception
6.Mutual Respect	6. Disrespect
7.Support	7. Neglect
8.Humility	8. Arrogance
9.Enjoyment	9. Mean-Spiritedness
10. Compassion	10. Callousness
11. Sharing/Caring	11. Selfishness/Egotism
12. Complimentarity	12. Negative Criticism
13. Security	13. Insecurity
14. Interdependence	14. Dependence
15. Spirituality	15. Non-Spirituality

(Reprint, Chapter VI, *Africana Womanist Literary Theory*, 2004, 79-97)

BIBLIOGRAPHY

Akbar, Na'im. "Materialism and Chauvinism: Black Internalization of White Values." In *Crisis in Black Sexual Politics*. Edited by Nathan Hare and Julia Hare. San Francisco: Black Think Tank, 1989.

Aldridge, Delores P. *Focusing: Black Male-Female Relationships*. Chicago: ThirdWorld Press, 1991.

"America's Wasted Blacks." *Economist* 318, 7700 (March 1991): 11-12.

Bâ, Mariama. *So Long a Letter*. London: Heinemann, 1989.

Belle, Yvonne; Bouie, Cathy; and Baldwin, Joseph. "Afrocentric Cultural Consciousness and Afrian American Male-Female Relationships." In *Afrocentric Visions Studies in Culture and Communication*. Edited by Janice Hamlet. Thousand Oaks, Calif.: Sage Publications, 1998.

Chapman, Audrey. *Entitled to Good Loving: Black Men and Women and the Battle for Love and Power*. New York: Henry Holt, 1995.

Fanon, Frantz. *Black Skin: White Masks*. New York: Grove, 1967.

Ferguson, Susan J. *Shifting the Center*. Mountain View, Calif.: Mayfield Publishing, 1998.

Gordon, Vivian. *Black Women, Feminism, and Black Liberation: Which Way?* Chicago: Third World Press, 1987.

Hare, Nathan. "The Black Coed Growing into Womanhood." In *Crisis in Black Sexual Politics*. Edited by Nathan Hare and Julia Hare. San Francisco: Black Think Tank, 1989.

Hudson-Weems, Clenora. *Africana Womanism: Reclaiming Ourselves*. Troy, MI.: Bedford Publishers, 1993.

Karenga, Maulana. *Introduction to Back Studies.* 2nd ed. Los Angeles: Calif.: University of Sankore Press, 1993.

Lourde, Audre, "Age, Race, Class, and Sex: Women Redefining Difference" In *Racism and Sexism: An Integrated Study.* Edited by Paula S. Rothenberg. New York: St. Martin's, 1988.

Madhubuti, Haki R. *Black Men: Obsolete, Single, Dangerous?* Chicago: Third World Press, 1990.

McMillan, Terry. *Disappearing Acts.* New York: Viking, 1989.

Miller, Jerome. "African American Males in the Criminal Justice System." *Phi Delta Kappa.* June 1997, Vol. 78 Issue 10: 1-13.

Reynolds III, A. L. *Do Black Women Hate Black Men?* New York: Hastings House, 1994.

Skwira, Gregory. "A Story Tightens as an Affair Unravels." *Detroit News.* Section M, Col. 2. 10 September, 1989, p. 2.

Staples, Robert. *The World of Black Singles.* Westport, Conn.: Greenwood Press, 1981.

CHAPTER SEVEN

In Response to Don Imus, 2007: Anti-Misogyny in Defense of the Africana Woman

". . . Nappy Headed Hos"

--DON IMUS

It is not so much the word "nappy" that we found offensive in Don Imus' widely televised, condescending ridicule of the Black basketball players at Rutgers University in 2007. It was the context in which that word was used, the so-called assignment of who we, as Black women are. The term "nappy" in and of itself is not negative. Quite the contrary, it is positive, authentic, and accurately descriptive, thus, making it very much accepted in the Black community, and particularly among Black youths today. Our hair has been often described as "nappy" or "kinky" or "very curly" and positive, proud Black women, and men, too, for that matter, have not taken offense to its use as a consciously warm assessment of our hair. With Imus, on the other hand, we are called "hos/whores" in a put-down, misogynistic fashion. The connotation is degrading, as it suggests that Black women are promiscuous and thus, deserving of being used, abused and called out of their names by any man, Black or white for that matter. Had we been called "Beautiful, nappy headed Black women," the whole controversy would have never happened.

There have been numerous books written by Blacks regarding the caring for natural Black hair, such as *Nappy Heads*. A number of children books, such as *Nappily Happy*, have been written with positive connotations of the term and there are a growing number of Black beauty solons across the nation, such as "Nappy by Nature" that promote and celebrate "nappy" hair as a symbol of beauty and authenticity for Black people. These natural hair salons, with every service imaginable for the caring of locks, comb coils/twists, braids, twist outs, and the long-standing afros are astounding. To be sure, because of our pride in ourselves and our looks, we resent the insults of Imus and those of others, like our unconscious Black brothers who put down their own Black women. The inherent disdain and even ridicule that went with what Imus said on live TV for all to hear represent the ultimate act of disrespect of Black women which must now come to a halt.

In the Foreword to the first edition of *Africana Womanism: Reclaiming Ourselves* in 1993, the late Dr. Zulu Sofola, Professor and Chair of the Department of the Performing Arts, University of Nigeria, Ilorin, who was distinguished as Nigeria' first female playwright, had the following to say about how the Western World had too often devalued the beauty and sanctity of the Black woman and Black womanhood:

> As a race the most painful part of our experience with the Western world is the "dewomanization" of women of African descent. It is true that to successfully destroy a people its female component must be first destroyed. The female gender is the center of life, the magnet that holds the social cosmos intact and alive. Destroy her, and you destroy life itself.

(Sofola, quoted in Africana Womanism, xviii)

The following are six (6) raps/poems I wrote in direct response to Don Imus in which I addressed both Black men and women relative to how we see and respect/disrespect ourselves and each other, and moreover, how we respond to the way others attempt to define and name us without permission:

For Black Men

1. LOVE AND RESPECT

Wonder why we imitate others' beauty?
It's 'cause you seek outside as your duty.
Wonder why we stoop so very hard to please?
It's 'cause you flee to others for your tease.

Black male-female relationships
History reveals was shaped from outside.
Black men were taught to hate our lips.
From whence comes power not to be denied.

Wonder why we imitate others' beauty?
It's 'cause you seek outside as your duty.
Wonder why we stoop so very hard to please?
It's 'cause you flee to others for your tease.

History reveals we protected all our men,
'Cause to protect us meant to risk their lives.
You were forced to shun our needs and not defend,
Your mothers, daughters and your precious wives.

Wonder why we imitate others' beauty?
It's 'cause you seek outside as your duty.
Wonder why we stoop so very hard to please?
It's 'cause you flee to others for your tease.

Conditioned not to love and respect us,
To see us other than true beautiful queens.
You looked outside to make a royal fuss
Over outside mates as beauties for you kings.

Wonder why we imitate others' beauty?

It's 'cause you seek outside as your duty.
Wonder why we stoop so very hard to please?
It's 'cause you'll flee to others for your tease.

2. IT AIN'T ALL GOOD

So only certain Black women are truly whores?
Others are working equals to you and yours
Okay then there is something in the name
But still it ain't all good with such a game.

Why can't we make those who are labeled dumb
Become the opposite of who they have become?
Let's make them want to not be a chicken-head.
But respected beautiful Black sisters instead

So only certain Black women are truly whores?
Others are working equals to you and yours
Okay then there is something in the name
But still it ain't all good with such a game.

Now look at us with new-found self esteem.
You thought we couldn't reverse the lower team.
Well, now you see how true beauty emerges
Since taking total control over all our urges.

So only certain Black women are truly whores?
Others are working equals to you and yours
Okay then there is something in the name
But still it ain't all good with such a game.

3. BACK IT UP

Back it up—
The booty shaking
The name calling

The fowl language and all.

The self hatred
The female bashing
The male bashing and all

The anti love
The anti family
The anti God and all.

The time has come,
Your love will flip--
The bottom will top for some.

4. GONE

Own up to all of your true prejudices
And we must also acknowledge our own.
The time is over now for hating on us.
The time for disrespect is truly gone.

Don't claim mistakes of modern hip-hoppers
As the real source of racist, bogus words.
Don't even try to cover up your fault
Which we must certainly now call to a halt.

Own up to all of your true prejudices
And we must also acknowledge our own.
The time is over now for hating on us.
The time for disrespect is truly gone.

5. NO HISTORY, NO BALANCE

Give me back my history; give me back my life,
Without these things there is no real balance.
Don't take my history, please don't crush my life.

Knowledge in the end will make the difference.

Did we just pop out to attack each other
Without the love for our sister and brother?
Then blaming the victim must be truly right
Since there's no history, no basis to frame our sight.

Give me back my history; give me back my life,
Without these things there is no real balance.
Don't take my history, please don't crush my life.
Knowledge in the end will make the difference.

6. Blessed Life

Life's for the living, so please let's live it now.
Enjoy the real fresh fruits of blessed life—
Love, happiness, respect and a little bow
To Jesus Christ who granted us this life.

Up and away—the joys are for us all.
The woes must vanish first before we fall.
Let's kick it now into the right directions.
Good times are ways to life-long connections.

Life's for the living, so please let's live it now.
Enjoy the real fresh fruits of blessed life—
Love, happiness, respect and a little bow
To Jesus Christ who granted us this life.

Let's kick it, all the way to true glory.
No need to avoid our much deserved fun.
Remember God does not believe in worry.
Now is the true time for true heavenly sun.

Life's for the living, so please let's live it now.
Enjoy the real fresh fruits of blessed life—
Love, happiness, respect and a little bow

To Jesus Christ who granted us this life.

I close this commentary on perceptions and misconceptions about Black women by both Black and white men. This is effectively done with a powerful poem, "It Ain't Easy Being a Queen," by the renown poetess, Sonia Sanchez, who continues her mission of speaking truth to her people, a mission she started over forty years ago during the celebrated Black Arts Movement of the searing sixties:

IT AIN'T EASY BEING A QUEEN

We black women have been called many things
Foxes, matriarchs, Sapphires, and recently . . . Queens
I would say that Black women have been a combination
Of all them words. . . 'cause if we examine our past history, at one
    Time or another, we've had to be like them words be saying,
But today, there are some words we can discard,
There be some we must discard,
For our survival, for our own sanity,
For the contribution we must make to our emerging Black nation.
And we must move as the only Queens of this universe
To sustain, to keep our sanity, in this insane, messed up . . .
Diet conscious, pill taking, masochistic,
Miss Ann oriented society
Got to be dealt with cause that's us.
Y'all hear me? US! Black Women!
The only queens of this universe
Even though we be stepping unqueenly sometimes
Like . . . It ain't easy being a Queen in this unrighteous world
    Full of . . .
Miss Anns and Mister Anns
But we be steady trying! (Cited in Noble 291)

Bibliography

Hudson-Weems, *Africana Womanism: Reclaiming Ourselves.* Troy, MI: Bedford, 1993.

Sanchez, Sonia quoted in Jeanne Noble. *Beautiful, Also, Are the Souls of My Black Sisters.* Englewood Cliffs, NJ: Prentice-Hall, 1978.

Sofola, Zulu. Foreword in *Africana Womanism: Reclaiming Ourselves.* Clenora Hudson-Weems. Troy, MI: Bedford, 1993.

Wheeler, Barbara. Quoted in *Contemporary Africana Theory, Thought and Action: A Guide to Africana Studies,* edited by Clenora Hudson-Weems. Trenton, New Jersey: Africa World Press, 2007.

CHAPTER EIGHT

Racism vs. Sexism/Obama vs. Clinton:
Human Survival/Economic Security via Unity or
Gender Divide

"I got your back, Boo"

--MICHELLE OBAMA, JUNE 3, 2008

The above are the memorable words of Michelle Obama, wife of the Nation's first Black Democratic Presidential nominee, Barack Obama, June 3, 2008. Bringing humanism back to the venue of the First Lady, and, in her case, the potential First Lady, Michelle, as she leaves the podium from the side of her husband of fifteen years, "fist bumps" and gives a "thumbs up" commitment of assurance to Barack. He, then, confidently moves to center stage to address his supporters, the American people, during his historical victorious moment of winning the nomination for the Democratic Party for President. This triumph is, indeed, a victory for all America, as Obama succeeds in breaking the racial barrier, at least for now and hopefully forever. For Michelle, a success in her own rights, an attorney and Harvard Law School graduate, along with her husband, she vows to remain there for Barack, as she has throughout their marriage. She is well aware, as well as he, that to weather the storms of life with an agenda that promotes our human rights to Equal pay and Health Care, and to persevere with ultimate success, it will take a collective effort on

129

the part of both genders to bring this thing to fruition. It is a struggle shared by both, ultimately bringing forth world harmony for the future of not only their children, but for all our children on the whole. Clearly Obama's struggle, and by extension that of all Americans, males and females alike, are one and the same--a battle for transcending the woes and limitations of our society to hold at bay any person, group or idea. In short, the fact that Obama, a Black man, succeeded in winning the Democratic nomination for the President of the United States of America strongly demonstrates the transcendence of race at this critical moment in history. The gender factor, represented in the campaign of Hillary Rodham Clinton, a herald for women's rights, indeed, a very critical issue today as in the past, far exceeds the race factor for her. Obama does not ignore gender issues, as he insists that Hillary's concerns are valid. Moreover, he always demonstrates love and respect for his wife as well as gives constant references to his two daughters and the hope for a better future for them as females, free from not only racial discrimination on all fronts, but misogyny as well. Still race reigns high as a number one hurtle in our overall success as an American people. Certainly fair game is penultimate during these critical times in American history when the economy, always interconnected with the race, and the gender factor, too, is without doubt in a serious tail spend today.

In a headline story, January 17, 2008, the following quotation makes a poignant commentary on the issue of racism versus sexism but ends on opening up these issues to a broader base, which contemplates additional issues for transcending those limitations:

> *Bruce Gordon, former president of the NAACP, said any suggestion that sexism had become a more oppressive bias than racism is a "huge overstatement." Both are alive and well, he said, "but it would be disappointing if in the course of this campaign the attention of the voting public shifts to gender and race instead of dealing with the substantive issues."*
> *(Crary, "Sexism vs. Racism," p. 1)*

Despite the fact the Obama initially tried to avoid race issues in his campaign early on, he was ultimately forced to do so. Therefore, let us start the dialogue by considering the obvious--racism versus sexism.

Given the current political climate, inescapably intertwined with the mounting threat of economic devastation the world over, one is boldly confronted with the idea of what is most critical for the survival of today's society, particularly for Africana people, the least favored in our society who should be thus, considered a priority in order to secure the birthright of all in the on-going struggle for total parity. At the center of the Democratic primary debate between Hillary and Barack was the question as to which candidate was most viable and as the former insists, "the most electable" for the 2008 Presidential Election. Within this context emerges the question, "Sexism vs. racism: which is more taboo?" The question is assessed following a feminist response to it earlier by one of the most noted white feminists today:

> *Feminist leader Gloria Steinem, argued in a New York Times op-ed last week, that gender is probably the most restricting force in American life—more so than race.*
> *But others involved in politics suggest the situation is more complex and that both race and gender are used to discriminate against people.*
> *(Crary, "Sexism vs. Racism," p. 1)*

Statistics has proven that there are more women victimized by gender subjugation than Blacks victimized by racial oppression, thus, indisputable. While women are among the majority group, the numbers of those discriminated against based upon their gender reflect both those in the already established majority group (whites) as well as those among the minority group (Blacks). Thus gender, not race, is the greater number because that group constitutes a compilation of both races. Be that as it may, the number alone does not equate the intensity or potency of the problem. True, there are less people affected negatively by racism than those negatively affected by sexism, but the degree to which gender negativity impacts is far less intense than one would imagine or care to admit. According to Linda LaRue,

> *Blacks are oppressed, and that means unreasonably burdened, unjustly, severely, rigorously, cruelly and harshly fettered by white authority. White women, on the other hand, are only*

suppressed, and that means checked, restrained, excluded from conscious and overt activity. And this is a difference. (218)

To be sure, racism, from its inception, is indisputably astounding. It is unspeakable and incomprehensibly debilitating, which has and continues to have an impact on all levels, indelibly impacting on the Black race one generation after another. In short, racial restitution is more compelling than the need for gender equity, although both are critical issues that unquestionably need to be properly addressed. Just resolving the gender problems does little to resolve the pervasive problems Black women face daily, as well as their male counterparts. Our problem, then, in many ways, is one and the same, and thus, "we cannot afford to divide on the gender line," which will leave the humongous race problem still unresolved. (Hudson-Weems)

And the debate continues. When Oprah Winfrey was asked how she could support a male candidate for presidency when we have a viable female candidate, her immediate response was "Because I'm free." Oprah's statement represents a double *entendre*, for while it connotes that her choice should not be limited on the basic of either her gender or her race, it also denotes that for her, as for Black people in general, the race factor is the most critical one, since the place for Blacks in general has been that of the bottom level on all spheres. The penultimate question, then, is this: How can we end, once and for all, this vicious cycle for Africana people? More to the point, how can we ensure that we, and more important, our future generations, do not continue to merely exist, but rather live a life of happiness, comfort and security, free from the threat of the abominable race, class and gender monster, whose very modus operandi is based upon none other than pure greed and groundless superiority, indeed, a pathetic act of concocted egotism? As I earlier proclaimed in the lead chapter in *State of the Race: Creating Our 21ˢᵗ Century: Where Do We Go from Here?*

> *. . . As we stand on the banks of the new millennium, none of the characteristics of the Africana woman, and the Africana man as well, are as critical here as the seminal feature of Africana women being In Concert with Males in the Liberation Struggle. Everything depends upon our collective struggle. Thus,*

> *collectivism as opposed to individualism is essential to Black survival. In returning to the collective struggle and leadership of Africana people for the survival of our entire family/.community, let us not forget our past strengths, indeed, the rich legacy of our glorious African ancestry. (Hudson-Weems quoted, 23-4)*

As an Africana womanist, I believe in the power of the word, hence, we need to speak into existence a fair, quality life for all, one in which humankind in general can co-exist, without conspiracy, selfishness or malevolence. Yes, there will be a time when all will have only a dominant common struggle with which to contend, for life itself is not perfect, as there will forever be things to improve upon. But for the moment, let us acknowledge and address without apologies our overall immediate concerns as a people, eliminating individual prioritization as a prerequisite before attempting to move on to that ultimate level. I propose that we first understand, appreciate, and openly acknowledge that unity is, indeed, a key factor in correcting societal ills, with the realization that struggle commands both genders to work together. This is not an exclusive gender battle, but rather a battle for the sanctity of life itself, indeed, the very foundation of the theory of Africana Womanism, my twenty-year commitment to the global Africana family. As stated in *Africana Womanist Literary Theory* (2004), the sequel to *Africana Womanism: Reclaiming Ourselves*, (1993) "It is even clearer that we as a people cannot afford to divide our energies and concerns along the popular gender line of feminism, so characteristic of the contemporary battle between the sexes within the dominant culture" (Hudson-Weems 39). Notably, because of the severity, pervasiveness, and life-threatening nature of racism, aspirations for racial parity, rather than female empowerment as an exclusive, should be the main emphasis for any and all of us, no matter the color, indeed, a priority that is so very much needed in order that we may all live together in harmony. If these issues are adhered to, we would be bearing witness to a powerful calling together of all people in an unselfish concerted struggle against oppression, including the social, political, psychological, economic, legal, spiritual, as well as our physical well-being and security today.

Africana Womanism, therefore, can be construed as a viable solution to one of today's biggest problems. The challenge is humongous. It will require that as an American people we open up our hearts to a broader communal, rather than an individualistic struggle. Whether or not we are ready to take that quantum leap into the beginning of the first day of the rest of our lives in a fair and just world, one in which only we can help bring into fruition, is up to us. The fact remains that it is important that each of us does our part in making a harmonious world, for if we fail to identify and help to correct the problem, it will surely go unchallenged and thus, will continue to reign and wreak havoc on our everyday lives forever. We must enter this struggle with the realizations that this, too, will surely come to past if we but just give it the attention it so desperately needs now.

The benefits are vast, as they are not only for Africana people. They are, without question, for us all, no matter the race, class, gender, etc. Unquestionably, everyone would be more content with the ideal--everybody's priorities being respected and properly dealt with for the ultimate experience of happiness, peace, and success. And the added bonus is that whether you are the victim or the victimizer, we will all greatly benefit. This is, indeed, an unexpected gift, particularly for the latter, who must understand that the gift can only be achieved through remorse and atonement, ultimately leading to final redemption. By now, we must be familiar with the old saying, redemption comes only through good deeds. Well then, let us seize the moment now to perform good deeds in the name of humanity. This could conceivable begin the reversal of the negative direction our world is going toward. Moreover, as for the victim, we must be willing to forgive all past injustices, as forgiveness is the primal step in the healing process, indeed, a transformation our society desperately needs.

Let us, then, as a people, begin by ending all forms of negative "isms" forever--racism, classism, and sexism, thereby allowing the commencement of the real struggle for all humankind. Clearly Obama and the American people are attempting to make that first giant step at this critical moment in American history. They are coming together during this presidential campaign and they are doing so at a much faster pace than people ever imagined. The real clincher is this: What does Obama's unannounced Urban Plan include for the American people? Will he illuminate and address key issues for the oppressed, underclassed, and minorities? One would hope so; however, the proof has not come forth as of yet, even though Obama does make reference to an Urban Plan. Those issues must include Mass Unemployment, Child Care, Universal Health Care, critical Food Shortages, affordable Higher Education, the Plight of Black Farmers and Land Owners, as well as Gentrification and the Housing crisis in general. If, indeed, he has these critical issues in his plan, if elected, he has the potential to be one of the greatest U.S. presidents ever, in restoring America's national pride and moreover, its global image and leadership. Look at God!:

Song of the Human Race

A long time ago in a little bitty place
On the great big continent of Africa,
Life had made it to the human race
And they all lived together in Africa.

Some decided to go
Some decided to stay.
Others went along
But stopped along the way.

Some walked to Europe and some kept the pace
Across the great big continent of Asia.
Others traveled across the Bering Strait
To North and South America.

Moving cross the land,
People in migrations.
Walking hand and hand
For many generations.

Years passed by and a little bitty ship
Crossed the great big Atlantic Ocean.
Other people made that long and daring trip
Cross the great big Atlantic Ocean.

Little did they know
They found their sisters and brothers.
From a long, long time ago
When they'd split up from the others.

Now we live in a little bitty space
On the continent of North America.
Our roots go back to that little bitty place
A long time ago in Africa.

"Oh Say Can't You See"
Our roots are from the same big tree
That crosses land and sea,
The one tree of humanity.

So sit right down in your little bitty space.
Be thankful for your friends.
Love every one in the human race
Because we're all true kin.
Because we're all true kin.

TERI LUCK McDUFFEY

CHILDREN SONG WRITER AND TEACHER

Bibliography

Asante, Molefi Kete. Quoted in his Afterword in *Africana Womanist Literary Theory.*

Trenton, New Jersey: Africa World Press, 2004.

Crary, David. "Sexism vs. Racism: Which Is More Taboo?" *Tri-State Defender*, p. 1. January 17, 2008.

Hudson-Weems, Clenora. "Africana Womanism: Entering the New Millennium.

Kamara, Jemadari and Tony Menelik Van Der Meer, editors. *State of the Race, Creating Our 21ˢᵗ Century: Where Do We Go from Here?* Boston, MA: Diaspora Press, 2004, 7-26.
_____. *Africana Womanist Literary Theory.* Trenton, New Jersey: Africa World Press, 2004.

LaRue, Linda. "The Black Movement and Women's Liberation." *Female Psychology: The Emerging Self.* Sue Cox, ed. Chicago: SRA, 1976. 216-225.

McDuffey, Teri Luck. *Song of the Human Race.* Unpublished, revised, 2008.

Chapter Nine

Conclusion
Authentic Existence, Racial Healing & Economic Security

MSNBC: As Senator Barack Obama opens his campaign as the first African American on a major party presidential ticket, nearly half of all Americans say race relations in the country are in bad shape and three in ten acknowledge feelings of racial prejudice, according to a new Washington Post-ABC News poll.

At the turn of the 20th century, Dr. W.E.B. DuBois prophetically announced in the last sentence of the first chapter of *Souls of Black Folk*, first published in 1903, that "The problem of the Twentieth Century is the problem of the color line" (DuBois 41). That problem has extended itself well into the 21st century and unless something powerful and spiritually happens, it will continue until perhaps even another century. This book culminates with the hope of turning that around for us, first by confronting "the true ugliness of American racism staring us right in the eye" (my statement on Emmett Till as symbol, quoted in Abdul-Jabbar's *Black Profiles in Courage*, p. 206), as well as the utter disrespect of Black women in Chapter Seven on Don Imus. Moving toward correcting the problem are the ideals in Chapter Eight on Barack Obama with the nomination of the country's first Black U.S. President nominee for the

Democratic Party. The book thus, appropriately closes with a positive political edge.

Chapter Seven makes a serious attack on the public image of Black women with Imus labeling the Black Rutgers University Basketball players "Nappy-Headed Hos" during his nationally-syndicated talk show, *Imus in the Morning*. His polar opposite, Barack Obama, interestingly evokes controversy on issues relative to Black people in general and their ability and experience, or the apprehension about the lack thereof, relative to holding a position of such high merit, the chief executive of this country. He is in the midst of the widely publicized controversy surrounding the Presidential election, which, among other things, debates the electability of Senator Obama, a young Black man of "too little experience" for the position of President of the United States of America.

Existing in a hostile, racist society, let us first look at the Black woman, certainly a concern during this historic election with an over-emphasis on Obama's wife at such an early stage of the campaign. Too much emphasis is being placed on her personality and her physical appearance as if she were the presidential candidate, so much so that Barack had to request that the media leave Michelle alone. Needless to say, the Black woman in general, like Michelle, as the culture bearer for her race, must nurture and guard her public personae against the throws of misogynist attacks. Her male counterpart, too, symbolizing the Black man and the Black race in general, is under close scrutiny as all candidates must be, and thus, he must carefully order his every step. This culminating focus is the story of the historic presidential election of Obama and his mission to bring about true unity among all Americans. It is his destined journey, with his wife at his side, who must together travel the road to economic security, racial healing and human survival for all America. As we all bare witness to and evaluate for ourselves the dynamics of this advent, it will be left up to us to positively receive and interpret it, with the knowledge that it is God who ultimately informs our thoughts and dictates our steps if we chose to be guided by the divine.

This book, loaded with complexities on many fronts, serves a two-fold purpose, which involves the political and private worlds of the American people. For example, the public dynamics were explored in the Obama story represented in Chapter Eight. Demonstrating the interconnection of the two worlds, I used the Africana Womanism template as a tool of analysis, thus, interpreting the convergent public and private worlds of the Africana man and woman, a model male-female interaction in general. The book opens with an historical account of the creation and evolution of a theoretical concept for the Africana Diaspora woman, and progresses to a delineation of her specific characteristics, and by extension those of her male counterpart. We witness how she operates within both her home and work environments, specifically how she interacts with her family, her friends and society on the whole. Moreover, we witness the Africana woman's acceptance of self in carrying out the dictates of her own culture. Finally, we see and feel her comfort in interacting with people and scenarios outside her own private domain, always insisting upon self-authentication for both inner peace and pride, and external appreciation. In other words, by being true to herself and her culture, she is able to find a comfort zone for herself, while at the same time, finding a level of societal respect, which makes more possible the realization of the recognition she deserves and the parity she demands on all fronts. This smooth movement from private to public domain is a natural journey for her, as well as for her male counterpart. She flows from within to without, from the public to the political arenas, which are forever challenging her totality.

In the end, whether the American people elect Senator Barack Obama, the Democratic nominee, or Senator John McCain, the Republican nominee, the motive behind that choice should not be based upon the age-old racism/sexism attitudes, but rather it must be based upon the hope for a quality life for all and for a war-free and financially secure society as well. To be sure, the American people want a president whose agenda promotes both unity among the races and the end of the long lived woes of life, resulting invariably in physical, psychological, economic, and material devastation. All that we can hope, vote, and pray for is someone committed to ameliorating this unfortunate circumstance. In the words of Nobel Prize-Winning author, Toni Morrison, "And isn't that exactly what every woman wants [for her family]...," every mother, daughter, wife, cousin, aunt, and friend? (Morrison, *Time Magazine*, 1989). The question is rhetorical, as the Africana womanist is always there, prominently and permanently placed in this picture, forever aspiring to divine love, true happiness and ultimate security via unity for all of God's people to experience. Pass it on! Pass it on! Pass it on!

Bibliography

Abdul-Jabbar, Kareem and Alan Steinberg. *Black Profiles in Courage: A Legacy of African American Achievement.* New York: William Morrow and Company, Inc., 1996.

DuBois, W.E.B. *Souls of Black Folks.* Greenwich, Conn: Fawcett Publications, Inc., 1961.

Morrison, Toni. *Times.* New York, 1989.

AFTERWORD

The political candidates for presidency of the United States of America cannot ignore the causes of the breakdown of domestic policy and the deterioration of America's status abroad. There has to be an institution designed to address such issues and concerns, and the Academy serves that purpose. More than ever, the Academy and its very raison d'être today are faced with a defining moment where its directions will dictate what kind of society we will be. Clenora not only gives us the rationale for CHANGE, but has given us a blueprint for turning the page with her books and political theory. Without question, the Academy in America not only dictates public policy, but it is the engine by which American Democracy survives. It pushes, as its thrust is the heartbeat of our very existence. Any free society must have an institution that will correct its course, no matter how painful its findings may be for the government to digest. (Below)

Higher Education is the cornerstone for research and development of all American Institutions. Nothing can escape its tentacle. Thus, the focus of public policy in an American Democracy seeking to eradicate the constitutional dilemmas of freedom, justice and slavery is to either eliminate the cause or to control the effect. After the Civil War, Congress extended full first class citizenship to the former slaves by enacting the Thirteenth, Fourteenth, and Fifteenth Amendments. In 1919 it extended full citizenship to white women and it was smooth and completely without problems. Unfortunately, the first class citizenship rights equal to that granted to the first citizens in 1787 did not result in the slave class being equal because American Democracy was afraid of creating an egalitarian society.

The debate over race, class and gender will go on as it should, but the historical record clearly points to second class citizenship for most African Americans. This historical fact can not be refuted. Dr.

Hudson-Weems points this out in all of her works, including this one, by emphasizing prioritization, rebuilding families, relationships, spirituality and communities. Her Obama piece, Chapter Eight of this book, hits the nail on the head. Black text/experience is real, as she states "there is a great difference between discrimination by privilege and protection, and discrimination by deprivation and exclusion." An egalitarian society where white supremacy is eliminated root-in-branch must be the ultimate goal. It is the only way the nation can be united and truly come together for the survival of not only our people, but the totality of humankind.

The political candidates for presidency of the United States of America cannot ignore the causes of the breakdown of domestic policy and the deterioration of America's status abroad. There has to be an institution designed to address such issues and concerns, and the Academy serves that purpose. More than ever, the Academy and its very *raison d'être* today are faced with a defining moment where its directions will dictate what kind of society we will be. Clenora not only gives us the rationale for CHANGE, but has given us a blueprint for turning the page with her books and political theory. Without question, the Academy in America not only dictates public policy, but it is the engine by which American Democracy survives. It pushes, as its thrust is the heartbeat of our very existence. Any free society must have an institution that will correct its course, no matter how painful its findings may be for the government to digest. Thus, in America, the Academy, the Avant Garde, as envisioned by Thomas Jefferson with the creation of the first public institution, the U. of Virginia, is the gate-keeper for American Democracy. It is supposed to be fully free and unfettered so that thought, however provocative, can prevail. Dr. Clenora Hudson-Weems is that step in the right direction towards this much needed egalitarianism in America.

ATTY. ALVIN O. CHAMBLISS, JR.

THE LAST ORIGINAL CIVIL RIGHTS ATTORNEY IN AMERICA

CHARLES HAMILTON HOUSTON CHAIR AT NORTH

CAROLINA CENTRAL UNIVERSITY SCHOOL OF LAW, 2006

EPILOGUE

ON BARACK AND MICHELLE OBAMA

I am looking for hope. I am looking to restore America's image to Americans and the world at large. I want to feel true pride in my country. Not in a wear-a-flag-pin, unconditioned way, but rightfully so. (Below)

I admit having two precocious youngsters may have caused my worldview to become less complex and more simplistic. I am looking for hope. I am looking to restore America's image to Americans and the world at large. I want to feel true pride in my country. Not in a wear-a-flag-pin, unconditional way, but rightfully so. The Obamas have two, precocious young girls of their own. Perhaps that is why their message of hope and "Yes We Can" has been cornerstones in Barack's campaign. (Below)

Hearing my four-year-old daughter speak about Barack Obama being a great man and "very nice" fills me with pride and wonderment. Of course, she constantly amazes me, being such a little smarty-pants... But the fact that she's speaking of the country's first honest-to-God potential African-American President equally blows me away. And while that monumental fact is mind-boggling for me, it's no more unusual for her than speaking about Backyardigan Uniqua being a mermaid. And why not? The future is full of limitless possibilities for an intrepid four-year-old. People fall into four categories for her: Nice, mean, girls and boys. A simplistic world-view, but a profound one...

Even though I'm far from four, I can relate to her questing spirit and hopefulness. I intend to nurture it in her and her sister. My mother instilled a "Can Do" spirit in my sister and me. It was one of her greatest gifts to us. I can only imagine how astounded and delighted she would be with Barack and Michelle Obama. I only wish she'd lived to see this historic election. We grew up in Gary, Indiana in the "Say it Loud, I'm Black and I'm Proud" era. I took Black pride to heart so much it was kind of a downer to have to switch up from saying Black people to African-Americans. I still interchange the labels to this day. Nevertheless, the pride and possibility remain the same for me, no matter what we call ourselves. And I must say I am exceedingly proud at this moment in time.

I don't know this as a fact, but, judging from Barack's campaign slogan "Yes, We Can," I imagine Barack and Michelle Obama grew up hearing "Can Do" messages from their family and/or teachers, just as I did. Children are not born feeling limited, they are, unfortunately, shaped into feeling limited. Those who "make it" have taken to heart Napoleon Hill's ageless expression, "Whatever the mind can conceive and believe, it can achieve." Some would argue, Barack wasn't supposed to be the Democratic nominee. He was a Junior Senator, and everyone truly expected this to be Hillary Clinton's moment. But he had the desire and the dream. He felt he could do it and he did. And even though Michelle reportedly was not, initially, chomping at the bit for Barack to run for President, I'll also wager she didn't question his dream, desire or ability to become the United States' first African-American President. Nor did she shrink from the possibility of being the country's first African-American First Lady and all that position entails... including being made a target.

Michelle Obama is an outspoken woman. She says what's on her mind and what's in her heart. And we all know these candid, heartfelt comments have been and continue to be taken out of context and overblown to outlandish proportions. Her every utterance is dissected and held up to such insane scrutiny that a Michelle Obama Watch blog-spot was initiated by prominent feminists to act as her media guard-dog. I checked out this blog-spot and recently found her senior year, 1985 Princeton Thesis, entitled "Princeton-Educated Blacks and the Black Community," in which she systematically analyzed Black students and alumnus experiences in a White Ivy League University and their relationship with the Black Community at large, had even been dug up, and the reporter cited her as a young woman grappling with her "blackness" in the elitist Princeton society. Actually, that was not the case. I read her impressive thesis. She was not grappling with her blackness. She was investigating a segment of African American students and alumnus of a particular institution and comparing their views relative to the Black Community pre-, during and post-Princeton. It was a brilliant, ambitious endeavor by a young, undergraduate senior. Pretty gutsy stuff, if you ask me. Not to mention a very worthwhile and noble undertaking. In this thesis, she shared a few personal observations which, of course, wound up being lifted and made to look as though they were the focus of her thesis. No matter. I'm actually glad the thesis is out there for all to see. Anyone who will take the time to read this provocative thesis will quickly ascertain how extraordinary this woman was and still is. Perhaps that's what shakes people up so about Michelle Obama. She is provocative. But she's also brilliant, dynamic, independent, gutsy, beautiful, stylish, loyal, loving, witty and real. And her husband is possibly the next President of the United States. By the way, the qualities I just cited are not only those I'd admire in a First Lady, but qualities I'd want my two little daughters to possess, as well.

It should not come as a surprise that racism has already made its unfortunate appearance in this election process. The sickness continues to plague our country. But it's heartening to see that the majority of American people seem more concerned with finding the person who can repair this broken country and deliver the cure, than what that person looks like. They are looking to Barack Obama. Indeed, Barack Obama has shocked his opponents by being embraced by all cultures, not just the African-American culture. But while negative attacks from his political opponents are to be expected, it is painfully and shockingly obvious how much of the mainstream media has joined the fray. They continue to lose credibility, journalistic integrity and respect by grasping for any thing to make the public believe Barack Obama cannot relate to whole groups of people because of who and what he is... On one hand, he's touted as an elitist. On the other hand, hateful, racist non-thinkers brand him as an undercover Muslim and prey on ignorant fears that he is somehow in league with terrorists. Whatever the toxic spin, the accusation is put forth that he could not be a President to all Americans. This is ironic on so many levels. What American President has ever related to everyone? Been embraced by everyone? And yet, what President has ever been the physical embodiment of such cultural diversity as Barack Obama? Is Barack Obama's unprecedented universal appeal making the media and his political opponents more desperate and more deplorable than ever? Absolutely! Will it get worse before it gets better? Probably! But I suppose this is progress, too. Change, like recovery from illness, is often painful. And the fever rages before it breaks.

Maybe America will finally turn into a "Can Do" country as opposed to a "Do whatever we want country." Having two daughters (aged four and nearly two), I deal with these behaviors on a daily basis. My four-year-old wants to do everything herself. "I can do it," is her constant cry while her younger sister still wants to do whatever she wants. As their parent, I have to monitor these impulses without crushing their spirits. It's my job to teach them about responsibility, consequences, consideration and making good choices. I want to instill in them the importance of kindness and keeping an open mind. And above all, I stress the need for them to use their words instead of resorting to physical violence. Real basic stuff, right? Right out of the parents' handbook. Then why, pray tell, has Barack had to endure tiresome criticism for being a great speaker and a visionary? Like these are bad things? Again, I have to wonder at the common sense of these critics. Since words are connected to thought, and thoughts are connected to deeds, exactly what is the problem?

I admit having two precocious youngsters may have caused my worldview to become less complex and more simplistic. I am looking for hope. I am looking to restore America's image to Americans and the world at large. I want to feel true pride in my country. Not in a wear-a-flag-pin, unconditional way, but rightfully so. The Obamas have two, precocious young girls of their own. Perhaps that is why their message of hope and "Yes We Can" has been cornerstones in Barack's campaign. Perhaps they are leading their children by example. These accomplished, loving parents have a spectacular legacy to leave. I only hope the American people, if not the World Community will also have the opportunity to benefit from their legacy, too. It's certainly been a long time coming.

CHARLOTTE GIBSON-BAUER

EMMY AWARD-WINNING TELEVISION WRITER &

PLAYWRIGHT, NEW YORK

About the Book

This book, advocating unity as a panacea for all societal ills, expounds on an authentic paradigm for all African Diaspora women, using *Africana Womanism* as a grid on which to erect their private and public personae. Done within the context of our cultural, historical matrix, the current controversial debates surround the historic presidential election. Beginning with a clear definition of the term, advocating the prioritization of race, class and gender as a workable strategy for ensuring total parity in a racist, classist and sexist world, the book ends with a collective struggle with men and women of all races, in a fashion which the Africana womanist has represented in her co-partnership with her male counterpart, a necessity for human survival of all people, since our destinies are, indeed, interconnected in a complex socio-political manner.

Africana Womanism and Race and Gender in the Presidential Candidacy of Barack Obama is the story of authenticity, human survival, economic security and racial healing for all America. Culminating in a political edge on the subject, it logically and convincingly moves from the proper naming and defining of the Africana woman in Part One, including identifying the 18 descriptors for the true Africana woman and her co-partner, to commentaries in Part Two on the biggest obstacle for Black people--racism. The book exposes how racism insidiously impacts upon personal and public relationships, such as the vicious assault on Black womanhood, misogyny, in the media by Don Imus. It continues with the race monster visibly "rearing its ugly head" in the current historical moment, as it unfolds in the ascendance of a Black man, Senator Barack Obama, to nominee for the Democratic Party for the President of the United States of America, surprisingly winning, to many, over Hillary Clinton, a white woman. Clearly the aspiration of the American people is the assurance of a better life for all, ensuring unity and financial security, no matter the race or gender of the selected head of state. That said, Barack has the potential to restore America's leadership once again in the world as well as ultimate global diplomacy.

About the Author

Clenora Hudson-Weems, Professor of English (UMC), received the PhD (U. of Iowa), M.A. (Atlanta U.), B. A. (LeMoyne College) degrees, and a Certificate of French Studies (L'Université de Dijon, France). She is author of *Africana Womanism: Reclaiming Ourselves* (Bedford, 1993); *Africana Womanist Literary Theory* (Africa World Press, 2004); two books in her Emmett Till Trilogy-- *Emmett Till: The Sacrificial Lamb of the Civil Rights Movement* (Bedford, 1994; AuthorHouse, 2006); *The Definitive Emmett Till: Passion and Battle of a Woman for Truth and Intellectual Justice* (AuthorHouse, 2006); and editor of the third of the Till Trilogy--*Plagiarism—Physical and Intellectual Lynchings: An Emmett Till Continuum* (AuthorHouse, 2007). She is also co-author with Wilfred D. Samuels of *Toni Morrison* (Prentice-Hall, 1990), and co-author with Dora Anderson of *The Rosa Parks of the Disabled Movement: Plantation Politics and a Black Woman's Struggle against General Motors, United Auto Workers and Government Bureaucrats* (AuthorHouse, 2008). She is editor of *Contemporary Africana Theory, Thought and Action: A Guide to Africana Studies* (Africa World Press, 2007). Forthcoming is her first novel, *Soul Mates*. She has completed a movie script, "Unearthing Emmett Till: Passion for Truth" (Barry Marrow, Oscar Award-Winning Co-Writer of *Rain Man* and Producer). Her current work is on the Plight of Black Farmers and Land Owners as an Emmett Till Continuum.

INDEX

R

race empowerment 45, 102
racial i, ii, 2, 13, 19, 20, 21, 60, 64, 100,
        101, 102, 110, 129, 130, 131,
        132, 133, 139, 140, 157
racism 18, 19, 21, 22, 23, 44, 57, 60, 65,
        76, 87, 100, 101, 108, 110, 113,
        114, 117, 130, 131, 132, 133,
        134, 140, 141, 149, 157
recognized 65
redemption ii, 134
Reid, Kathy Kravitz ii
Relationships ix, 10, 40, 48, 76, 99, 102,
        118, 119
remorse 134
Republican 141
respected 23, 44, 53, 74, 77, 78, 81, 89,
        124, 134
respectful of elders 44, 53, 111
responsibility vii, 53, 62, 68, 74, 76, 79,
        86, 93, 150
Reynolds III, A. L. 120
Rosa Parks of the Disabled Movement,
        The ii, v, 159
Rutgers University 121, 140

S

Samuels, Wilfred D. v, 159
Sanchez, Sonia 128
Sarpong, Antoinette Alexander ii
self-definer 43, 53, 56
self-esteem 58, 65, 91, 93, 94, 106, 117
self-namer 54, 73
Seven Deadly Sins 90
sexism ix, 10, 28, 65, 76, 99, 101, 120,
        129, 130, 131, 137
Shakespeare, William 97
Silence 34, 35
sisters ii, 56, 64, 88, 89, 91, 92, 93, 94,
        95, 96, 124, 136
Skwira, Gregory 120
Smith, Linda Anderson 50
Sofola, Zulu 128
South Africa ii, 38

So Long a Letter 4, 75, 82, 97, 99, 119
Spillers, Hortense 36
spiritual i, 5, 44, 53, 66, 67, 80, 111, 133
Staples, Robert 120
Steady, Filomina Chioma 13, 54
strong ix, 6, 16, 30, 44, 53, 64, 75, 78,
        87, 89, 100, 101, 111
Sula 85, 97
survival ii, vii, 2, 6, 21, 23, 27, 35, 45, 47,
        55, 57, 58, 60, 61, 64, 66, 69, 74,
        79, 80, 86, 101, 103, 109, 113,
        114, 115, 116, 127, 131, 133,
        140, 146, 157

T

terminology 19, 20, 22, 23, 28, 29, 30,
        31, 33, 34, 45, 46, 74
Texas Southern University 6, 7, 37
Thinker x, 37
Thompson, Bet ty Taylor 43
Till, Emmett Louis vii, 100
Time Magazine 35, 142
Toni Morrison v, 4, 35, 43, 48, 65, 70,
        72, 75, 85, 142, 159
transformation 134
Tri-State Defender 137
tripartite 23, 106
triple plight 23, 29, 108, 116
Truth, Sojourner 25

U

United Nations 39
United States iv, 9, 39, 101, 130, 140,
        145, 146, 148, 149, 157
unity 2, 10, 129
Universal Health Care 135
University of Iowa vii, 28

V

Van Der Meer, Tony 49, 137
victimization 22, 57, 93, 110
Villarosa, Linda 97
Vinyard, Alma 11
voice 18, 22, 34, 41

W

Y